# BUSINESS OPPORTUNITIES

## Teacher's Book

Anna Phillips

Terry Phillips

Oxford University Press

Oxford University Press
Great Clarendon Street, Oxford OX2 6DP

Oxford  New York
Athens  Auckland  Bangkok  Bogota  Buenos Aires
Calcutta  Cape Town  Chennai  Dar es Salaam
Delhi  Florence  Hong Kong  Istanbul  Karachi
Kuala Lumpur  Madrid  Melbourne  Mexico City
Mumbai  Nairobi  Paris  Sao Paulo  Singapore
Taipei  Tokyo  Toronto  Warsaw

and associated companies in
Berlin  Ibadan

OXFORD and OXFORD ENGLISH are  trade marks of
Oxford University Press.

ISBN 0 19 452029 3

© Oxford University Press 1994

First published 1994
Fifth impression 1998

Printed in Hong Kong

*Design* by Sarah Tyzack

# Contents

# Introduction

## Using the Course

*Business Opportunities* is designed for groups of intermediate learners. The book can also be used as a revision course, or to follow on from the *Business Objectives* course.

*Business Opportunities* can be used in two ways:

1   As a continuous course, to be used from start to finish. *Business Opportunities* starts with simpler structures and vocabulary and progresses to more complex language. Using the book in this way will enable students to gain a good basic working knowledge both of English grammar and of business vocabulary.

2   As a resource to be dipped into. Each unit is free-standing. There is no storyline or background information that has to be explained before individual activities are used. Using the book in a flexible manner will enable teachers to cater for the specific priorities of different groups. For example, engineers may be especially interested in Unit 11 (Products and Services); financial specialists may be more interested in Unit 9 (Reporting on Progress).

## Format of units

All fourteen units follow a broadly similar format.

### PRESENTATION

Key language points are presented in the form of a listening text. The material is generally exploited in the following ways:

*Listening for content:*   The teacher plays the taped conversation right through. A task-based activity helps students follow the gist of the conversation and pick up specific points of information.

*Listening for language*: In this phase the focus shifts to the forms of the language. The dialogue is replayed while students complete exercises designed to highlight specific words and phrases.

### LANGUAGE WORK

This section provides controlled practice of the target language in each unit. Some written exercises are included, but the emphasis is on oral practice. Many of these activities involve work in pairs and small groups. This has the advantage of maximizing the amount of practice that students get. Students who have not experienced this type of practice before may be worried about making mistakes and may require reassurance. You should monitor the pair and small-group work closely and encourage students to ask for help when necessary.

### SKILLS WORK

This section includes a speaking task along with a reading, writing, or listening task.

The speaking tasks here represent the culminating challenge of the unit. They are generally freer than the speaking practice in the LANGUAGE WORK section. They are also more demanding: students will need to draw on all their linguistic resources, as well as on the language just learnt. It is important that students do not feel they have failed if they make linguistic mistakes in these activities. Success here should be judged on communicative effectiveness rather than structural accuracy.

These tasks will often involve students in expressing their own ideas and opinions and giving accounts of events in their own workplaces. In this way, the activity and language employed will relate to the students' individual needs and experience. It is often a good idea for your students to have time to prepare these speaking activities. You may also wish to allow time at the end for questions and problems to be aired, for good language and communication practice to be praised, and for difficulties with performance to be identified and corrected.

The reading and listening texts in this section are accompanied by task-based comprehension activities, plus discussion and/or vocabulary work. The texts are generally longer and more difficult than elsewhere and students may encounter new language items not previously practised. At this stage, however, a passive knowledge is all that is required. Complicated explanations should not be necessary.

Practice is also provided in writing business letters, faxes, and reports. Managers who enjoy plenty of secretarial help may prefer to miss out these activities.

## Pronunciation and vocabulary

Every unit of *Business Opportunities* contains a pronunciation exercise with an accompanying taped recording. Every unit also contains at least one vocabulary exercise. The pronunciation and vocabulary exercises appear at varying stages of the unit and are listed in the index of the Student's Book.

## Appendices

### Role-play Notes

Some activities in the book require pairs of students to exchange different sets of information. In these cases, data is provided in files at the back of the student's book (pages 150–59). The files also contain extra information and answers for some activities.

### Tapescript

Exercises which are accompanied by tape recordings are indicated with a cassette symbol. ▭ A script is located at the back of the book (pages 160–69).

### Grammar and Usage Notes

Notes on the forms and functions of grammatical structures, functional phrases, information on letter and fax layout, and a list of irregular verbs, are located at the back of the Student's Book (pages 170–188). You may wish to draw students' attention to this reference resource at the beginning of the course.

### Glossary

The Student's Book also includes a glossary with explanations in English (pages 189–191).

### Learner Training

Business English students are invariably short of time and it is vital that they make efficient use of the precious study time they have available. For this reason, *Business Opportunities* contains many activities designed to encourage students to maximize their opportunities for learning and to develop the skills they need to study efficiently and independently. They include: Time Management (page 11), Recording Vocabulary (page 30), Using a Dictionary (page 63), and Guessing Unknown Words (pages 116–117).

## Teaching Business English

*Business Opportunities* has been designed to meet the practical needs of the numerous business English teachers whose specialist knowledge and direct experience of the business words is not extensive. Two elements in particular have shaped its approach:

1 *Authenticity of materials*
Documentation from real firms has been used to ensure business authenticity and relevance.

2 *Drawing on the students' professional expertise*
Many activities involve students in relating and discussing their own business experiences to ensure they contribute directly to the course content. This may mean that you will not always be in a position to supply the specialist terms the students need. This should not be a major problem, provided that you make clear your limitations at the start of the course. On balance, the benefits of encouraging students to discuss their 'real-life' business experiences far outweigh any drawbacks.

Obviously it is not possible for you to draw on your students' work experiences if you are teaching pre-experience students. For this reason, some alternative activities are provided in this book for teachers working with students who have not yet embarked on their business careers.

Alternative activities for pre-experience students are indicated with this symbol PX .

The subsequent pages of this book provide more detailed help with exercises, as well as notes on aspects of language. They also contain answers to activities and exercises in the Student's Book. You should be able to find these answers quickly and easily, thanks to the following design features.

**Answers to Student's Book activities all appear in this distinctive typeface.**

A cross-reference to the correponding pages in the Student's Book is provided at the top of every page of the Teacher's Book.

## PRESENTATION

> **Optional equipment and materials**
>
> *classes of six students or more:*
>
> Pieces of string/wool about I metre long; one for every two students

**I** Introduce yourself to the students using as many of the phrases in exercise 1 as is realistic. If students arrive late during or after your introduction, ask the other students to introduce you.

Students look at the six photos on pages 6–7 and see how much information they can work out from them before they read the texts: e.g., possible ages, jobs, nationalities.

Students read the introductions silently, or you read aloud with students following in the book, or choose individual students to read introductions aloud while class follows. Throughout the course, use these alternatives as appropriate.

Ask:
*What different ways are used to start the introductions?*
*How do they give their names?*
*What different ways do they use to describe their jobs?*

Students repeat some of the phrases after you.

Highlight prepositions (these will be a problem for most students) and verb forms as follows:

> I work **in** .....(name of town/department)
> I work **for** .....(name of organization)
> I'm based **in** .....(name of town/country)
> I am responsible **for** .......
> I'm in charge **of** ... **+ -ing**
> It's my job **to** ... (**do**)

Point out that all verbs are in the present simple tense for permanent jobs, e.g., I *travel* a lot.

Point out that the style is formal in these introductions; with one or two possible exceptions.

In small classes students can now introduce themselves to each other.

Large classes now get out of their seats and go to the centre of the room. Hold up the pieces of string in the middle of their lengths. Each student takes hold of one end. Let go of the string and ask the students to find their partner. They can then introduce themselves.

Students introduce their partner to other members of the class.

Monitor if feasible: walk round and listen unobtrusively and make a note of any errors in grammar, pronunciation, and style, but do not interrupt. When the students are back in their seats, go through the errors you noted.

**2** ▭ Students read the instructions and look at the task.

Check they all understand what to do. (Do this throughout the course.)

Play conversation 1 twice, then let students compare their answers in pairs. Do not confirm or correct answers yet, but play the relevant section of the cassette again if students are obviously having difficulty.

Repeat the procedure with conversations 2 and 3.

Ask students to find the tapescript on page 160.

Play the cassette again so that students can listen and follow the script. Students correct their answers.

Finally, as a double check, elicit correct answers, referring to the tapescript if necessary if there are still any misunderstandings.

NOTE: Alternative procedures for listening activities are given in later units.

**ANSWERS**

| Conversation I | Conversation 2 | Conversation 3 |
|---|---|---|
| Yes | Yes | No |
| Airport | Projection room | Alicante |
| Mr Jensen (Danish) | Signora D'Amore (Italian) | Juan Carlos (Spanish) |
| Joséphine Marca (French) | Dieter Nitte (German) | Mr Shingu (Japanese) |

**3** Check students understand the instructions. Go through the example with them. If necessary, do the first few sentences of the exercise with the students as examples.

Students can complete the exercise in pairs.

Elicit correct answers and discuss. Tell students not to worry if they cannot name the tenses: more details on the grammar will be given in future lessons. Point out that the name of the tense does not always tell you what time is referred to, e.g., the present continuous can refer to the present and the future.

If time is short, allocate two sentences to each pair of students. Each pair reports back to the rest of the class.

**ANSWERS**

| | | | |
|---|---|---|---|
| **1** | past and present | **9** | future |
| **2** | past | **10** | future |
| **3** | future | **11** | past |
| **4** | present and future | **12** | present |
| **5** | future | **13** | future |
| **6** | present | **14** | present |
| **7** | past and present | **15** | present and future |
| **8** | present and future | | |

# LANGUAGE WORK

**Equipment and materials**

Students' own business cards

Gapped text for exercise 1, page 10

KEY LANGUAGE POINT: The focus here is on everyday question forms which students generally find complex. The exercises are open-ended and flexible, so can easily be adapted to suit the level of the class. For example, exercise 1 could elicit a simple *What's your name?* from a lower level or slower class. However, more proficient students could be encouraged to use more subtle language, such as *I'm afraid I didn't quite catch your name earlier* or *Sorry, what was your name again?*

## Getting acquainted

**1** Students look through the prompts and think about the questions they could ask.

Elicit possible questions for the first two prompts only. Encourage higher-level classes to think of more polite and possibly more realistic questions as described above. Questions will mostly be in the present tense, except when certain polite forms are used.

Ask students to repeat the questions after you, then select one or two students to ask the questions and another one or two to answer.

Write the questions on the board for students to copy. Highlight problem grammar and pronunciation areas, especially the use of the auxiliary *do* in simple present questions.

Repeat the above procedure for the questions about companies and jobs.

Clean the board. Students work in pairs. Ask them only to use the prompts in their books if necessary.

Encourage students to add their own questions. Monitor (see exercise 2 above).

**POSSIBLE ANSWERS**

Sorry, I didn't quite catch your name earlier.
Where exactly do you come from?

What exactly does your company do?
Who are your main customers?
Who would your main competitors be?
Where is your company based?

What's your job title, exactly?
Which department are you in?
What are you responsible for?

**PX** Give pre-experience students the following tasks to do:

Find out
*   your partner's name
*   where they come from

Find out about their free time.
*   their family
*   their hobbies and interests
*   sports they play or watch

Find out about the course they are taking.
*   course title
*   the qualification it leads to

- department/faculty
- course component/subjects

**2** Use the same procedure, highlighting the grammar of past tense and present perfect questions.

**PX** With pre-experience students, get them to find out

- how long they have been studying here

- what school they went to before this one

- about the last time they used English. (When was it? Who did they talk to or write to? What was it about?)

- where they have learnt English in the past

**3** Use the same procedure, emphasizing the use of *will* for future predictions.

**SOME POSSIBLE ANSWERS**
Who will you need to attend meetings with?
What will they be about?
Who will you make phone calls to?
Who will you make presentations to?
What kind of deals will you negotiate?
Who will you show around? What type of technical machinery will you need to describe?
What kind of figures will you need to discuss?
What will you need to read?
Who will you socialize with?

Ask students to bring their business cards for the next lesson (Executive titles).

**PX** With pre-experience students, get them to find out:
- what they want to do after this course
- about the job they hope to have

Find out what they will have to do in English in their job. Do they think they will have to:

- attend meetings
- make phone calls
- make presentations
- entertain foreign guests and visitors
- describe technical machinery or processes
- discuss figures
- read reports and correspondence
- write letters, faxes and reports?

SUPPLEMENTARY ACTIVITY: Students write a short paragraph about either themselves or someone they have interviewed, based on the answers to the questions above. This can be done in class or for homework. Collect the work in: this will help you to find out more about your students' backgrounds as well as to see the standard of their written English.

## Executive titles

**1** Elicit answers and discuss.

Read the introductory text aloud; students follow in their books.

Check students understand *confused, compiled, recruitment agency, consistent,* and *strange mixture.* (Meanings should be clear from context.)

**2** Students discuss the answers in pairs, or you elicit answers from the whole class.

**3** Show students the first two verbs in the text. (*to act, to direct*)

Set a time limit for finding the rest of the verbs. Elicit answers and check students understand the verbs as you go along.

Go through pronunciation of the infinitive of the verbs paying attention to stressed syllables:

di<u>rect</u>
<u>or</u>ganize
lead
de<u>vel</u>op
main<u>tain</u>
es<u>tab</u>lish
repre<u>sent</u>
co<u>or</u>dinate
as<u>sist</u>
<u>ma</u>nage

Elicit an example sentence for each verb and ask the whole class to repeat and practise it. Or, for a more student-centred technique, allocate one or two verbs to each student (depending on numbers) and ask them to write a sentence with it. Students read their sentence aloud, then other students listen and correct if necessary. Students repeat and practise the sentence. Divide students into groups. One student at a time describes their jobs using the verbs above.

Go round and check students are using the correct tense.

Students can write a paragraph about their jobs using the verbs above. Collect written work in. Read two or three aloud to the rest of the class; students guess who wrote the paragraph.

NOTE: *Responsible* is an adjective followed by *for* or *to*. Check students understand the difference by asking

*What are you responsible for?*
*Who are you responsible to?*

Some languages have words similar to *responsible* that can be used as a noun. If this is the case with your students, point out we cannot say 'responsibles' in English meaning 'the people who are responsible for things'.

## Management styles

1 Ask students to think about the last two questions while they read.

Students can discuss their answers in pairs and ask you any questions on vocabulary they may have. Point out the use of the present simple verbs in the text.

With slower classes, provide students with a photocopied gapped text with all the simple present verbs missing. Students write in the missing verbs.

2 Elicit possible questions for each prompt from the class first as examples. Practise them if necessary. Students can then ask and answer in pairs. Check students are using 3rd person forms of the present simple tense correctly, e.g., *Where does he live? How often does he hold board meetings?*

If your class has difficulty, you can provide them with answers to which they must devise questions, e.g.,

Q What *time does he start work?*
A Around eight a.m.
Q How *many employees has he got?*
A 10,000.

3 Ask one pair to demonstrate the activity. Ask the rest of class to listen and correct any mistakes. Students work in pairs or groups of three. Monitor. Give students the correct version either orally or on the board, highlighting the language. Get students to repeat the sentences again, or give you more examples either orally or in writing. Alternatively, give students the incorrect phrases you heard and ask them to correct them.

Remember in feedback to focus on pronunciation, vocabulary, and appropriateness as well as grammar.

## Time management

1 Tell students there are no 'right' answers to these questions; the aim is to help them make the most of their course.

Students discuss answers (in pairs, groups, or as a whole class) and report back their findings to you and the rest of the class.

Suggest newspapers and books for students to read. Remind them of the times of TV and radio programmes in English. If your students are studying in the UK, recommend programmes that may be of interest. Children's news programmes and documentaries are easy to start with.

2 Elicit some examples for each sentence before asking students to write sentences. Go round and help: *I'm going to, I plan to, I intend to,* sound the most definite.

## Jobs Quiz

1 With students' books closed, write the four personality type headings on the board.

Ask students to predict information to go under each heading. This could be done in pairs or groups with a different heading allocated to each. Students read and check their ideas with the 'personality type' texts at the bottom of Student's Book page 12.

Tell students they are now going to find out their 'personality type'

Students could turn the statements in the book into questions to ask each other, e.g.,

9

1 *Would you love to do a parachute jump?*
2 *Do you like telling other people what to do?*

Go round during the activity and help with any difficult words/phrases, e.g., *to volunteer opinions, to set objectives* , etc. Questioner and respondent should swap roles.

**2** If necessary, demonstrate with one pair of students. Ask students if they agree/disagree with the analysis of their personalities. Point out the use of simple present verbs again.

### Employment

**1** Point out that students may be able to work out the meaning of words during the activity. When working through the answers, point out that most are alternative ways of saying the same thing, some more formal than others. But *retire* and *receive a pension* are two parts of the same process.

**ANSWERS**
Road 1: take on staff, recruit staff
Road 2: hand in your notice, resign
Road 3: retire, receive a pension
Road 4: be unemployed
Road 5: make staff redundant
Road 6: dismiss staff, fire staff, sack staff

NOTE: *Redundant* is an adjective usually used with the verb *make*; it is often used in the passive voice, e.g., *He's been made redundant. Sack* and *fire* are informal; *dismiss* is formal.

**2** As Student's Book

## SKILLS WORK

### Speaking

**1** Check students understand the instructions. Go round and check students are not listing too few or too many people.

**2** Go through the example sentences given in the Student's Book; ask students to underline the verbs and say what tenses they are in and why. Elicit examples for points 1, 2, and 3 and ask the whole class to repeat them after you. Encourage students to look back at the section on job titles to help them. Monitor while students do the activity.

### Listening

**1** Ask students to read the introduction.

Check comprehension by asking

*What is Schering?*
*What is their business exactly?*
*What has their French pharmaceutical subsidiary recently done?*
*What is one of the managers doing?*
*Who is he talking to?*
*Where are they from?*

Check students understand the task, then play the cassette all the way through. Students compare answers in pairs. If necessary, play the cassette, pausing after the relevant section for each answer, and students compare answers again. Elicit correct answers: be prepared to play relevant sections again if students have no answer or incorrect answers.

**ANSWERS**
Production Director
Personnel Manager
Work Groups: Manufacturing, Sales

**2** Students read the questions. Play the cassette, pausing after each relevant section. Continue as in 1.

**ANSWERS**
1 General Manager (Development and Marketing)
2 General Manager
3 Two are responsible for domestic sales, and one for foreign sales.
4 They can develop specialized knowledge; they help to motivate staff; they include a wide range of expertise.

Play the cassette once more with students following the tapescript on page 160. This helps students understand why they got answers right or wrong, it relates 'sight and sound', and it helps slow readers to speed up.

**3** Read the instructions aloud to the students and check they understand.

Explain that this activity revises all the language learnt in this unit and practises speaking fluently. Ask students to spend a few minutes looking back over the unit and checking their notes. Monitor to prepare for the activity, but do not interrupt or correct.

If you can record or video the exercise, play it back afterwards so students can correct themselves.

Monitor students as they draw their organigrams and give feedback as described above.

SUPPLEMENTARY ACTIVITY: Students make poster-sized organigrams for the classroom walls and/or write a short paragraph describing their organization.

## Pronunciation ▭

Ask students to say the word *organization* with the correct stress.

Ask them to identify the stressed syllables in words 1–10 .

Play the cassette or say the words yourself for students to make any necessary changes. Students compare answers in pairs. Elicit correct answers and play the cassette or say the words once more with students repeating.

**ANSWERS** are on Student's Book, page 161.

CLOSURE: The following procedure should be followed at the end of each unit:

**a** Remind students what they have learnt in the unit, referring to the tasks listed on Student's Book unit header page.

**b** Use what they have learnt in this unit in a free discussion.

**c** Get students to discuss/write down what they think they have learnt and then go through the points with them.

# PRESENTATION

> **Optional equipment and materials**
>
> Jigsaw pieces for exercise 3, page 12
>
> OHT of Vocabulary from opening activity
>
> Set of Dictionaries for opening activity
>
> OHT of itinerary for Listening
>
> Handout with gaps for Grammar Summary or OHT of Grammar

**1**   Pre-teach/check vocabulary. Put these pairs of words on the board or OHT:

| | |
|---|---|
| arrangements | appointments |
| itinerary | agenda |
| conference | meeting |

In pairs, students discuss the differences in meanings. Each pair explains one set, others confirm/correct.

NOTE: arrangements covers all types of planning, whereas appointments is only for meetings with people — usually one-to-one meetings.

**PX** Dictionary work is an alternative procedure for pre-teaching vocabulary.

1   Allocate a different pair of words to each pair of students

2   Give out dictionaries.

3   Feedback: each pair reports their findings to the rest of the class.

Practise pronunciation by spending a short time on the more difficult words and marking where the stressed syllables are on the board:

ar__rang__ements   ap__poin__tments   i__tin__erary   a__gen__da   __con__ference   __meet__ing

Also focus on:

— missing syllable in: arrang(e) ments; itiner(a)ry ; conf(e)rence

— *sch* /ʃ/ in schedule

— consonant clusters in appointments: *ntm /ə/ nts*

Before students read the 'Powerglide systems memo',

go through the heading and check students understand the information; also check students understand all the important vocabulary: *preliminary*, *workshop*, *tour*, *plant*, etc. Use 'Reverse Dictionary' method, e.g., *Which word means 'factory'?*

Explain the task: students will hear Emma Wood talking to three people: Ernesto Garrone, Kjell Olaffsson, and Michael Black. During the phone calls the itinerary will be changed. Students must change the itinerary as necessary during listening.

Do the first schedule change with the students as an example. If necessary, play the conversations more than once, pausing when appropriate.

**ANSWERS**

**A**   Arrival at 11 o'clock, not 10

**B**   Bringing a colleague, Signora Agnelli

**C**   Demonstration of the rolling mill for Agnelli at 2.00 on Thursday

**D**   Workshop tour at 3 o'clock, not 2.30

**E**   Kjell Olaffsson can't make lunch, but Louise Harvey still can

**F**   Friday breakfast meeting with Kjell Olaffsson at 8.30 at the Dorchester

**2**   The aim here is to encourage students to predict the language required to complete each conversation. It is important that the teacher does not correct or give feedback for the above activities yet — see Listening below.

Conversation 1:   Students fill the gaps individually, then compare answers in pairs .

Conversation 2:   Students fill the gaps in pairs.

Conversation 3:   Teacher elicits possible answers but does not confirm or deny.

Students then listen and correct their own answers.

Play each conversation, pausing and repeating as necessary.

**ANSWERS**

**1**   Who's calling, please?; put you through; ...anything else?; Let me know; until...then; meeting everyone; calling

**2**   Going to; how about; would; Shall we say?

**3**   is bringing; showing; not at all; would suit; Would you prefer?

Supplementary activities could include:

1 Students listen to the complete conversations again.
2 Pick up on specific features by following the conversation with the tapescript
3 Act out short sections of the conversations in pairs.
4 Write out the changed itinerary on a new memo.

**3** KEY LANGUAGE POINT: Stress that *would* is often used in polite phrases to replace more informal ones, e.g., *Can I / She wants / Do you want / That is...*

Ask students to underline *would* in the three conversation excerpts on pages 16 and 17. The examples they should find are:

1 I'd like to speak to Emma Wood
2 Yes, that would be possible
3 Would you mind showing her the rolling mill?
4 When would suit you best?
5 Would you prefer the morning or the afternoon?

Give examples of alternatives to prompt the more polite *would* answer, e.g., *I want to speak... Can you show her? When do you want to show her?*

Students do exercise 3 in pairs.

NOTE: Students often find matching tasks easier if the sentences are retyped and cut up into slips of paper which they can move around on their desks.

**ANSWERS**
1 e   2 d   3 b   4 c   5 a   6 f   7 g

Practise pronunciation. Students repeat some of the sentences chorally then individually, paying attention to:

1 *Would you mind if I brought a colleague with me?*
(linking and intonation)
2 *Would you like me to put it on the schedule?*
(linking and intonation)
3 *That'd be fine* — weak form /əd/
4 *Would you prefer the morning or afternoon?*
(stress and intonation)

**4** KEY LANGUAGE POINT: Check/revise present continuous form for positive, negative, and interrogative by asking questions about Mr Garrone's itinerary, e.g.,

*When is he arriving?*
*Who is he seeing at 4.30?*
*Is he having lunch at the Eight Bells?*

Get students to ask you questions in the same way.

Present the contrast between *was doing/is doing now*.

a Draw the following chart on the board

| Arrangement | |
|---|---|
| *Old* | *New* |
| arrival: 10.00 | arrival: 11.00 |

b Ask: *How can we talk about the old arrangement?*
Target: He *was* arriving at *10.00.*

c Ask: *How can we talk about the new arrangement?*
Target: *Now* he's arriving at *11.00.*

Students copy the chart into their books, then find and fill in more examples of changed arrangements by reading the transcripts and the itinerary in 1.

Ask about items which have changed. Students answer with target form, e.g.,

Teacher: *When's he arriving?*
Student: *He was arriving at ten, but now he's coming     at eleven.*

NOTE: Point out words that need to be stressed for contrast: *was...ten.../...now...eleven.*

In pairs, students ask and answer in the same way, using their charts as a guide.

# LANGUAGE WORK

---

**Optional equipment and materials**

OHT of Starting and finishing calls

OHT of exercise 2, page 14

Sets of coloured paper for Freer Practice Activity

Jigsaw of Conversations 1 and 2

---

## Polite questions

1 KEY LANGUAGE POINT: Refusing a request or offer is more difficult than agreeing. Refusals are usually followed by an explanation, e.g., *I'm too busy, I need it myself.*

Select two or three requests/offers using *would* from the previous lesson, write them on the board (or use an OHP) and elicit polite ways of agreeing or refusing. Add the students' suggestions to the board as in the plan below.

---

1 Would you put it on the schedule?
REQUEST

| AGREE | REFUSE |
|---|---|
| Yes, certainly | I'm afraid that would not be possible, there won't be time. |
| Yes, that would be possible. | |
| No problem. | That would be rather difficult, I'm afraid. |
| That would be fine. | |

2 Would you like me to arrange a demonstration?
OFFER

| AGREE | REFUSE |
|---|---|
| That would be very kind. | Thank you, but I won't have time. |

---

Focus on meaning by referring students to the example in the book using *Would you mind...?* and eliciting ideas. After some time, confirm that B agreed, then ask: *How does 'No' mean the same as 'Yes'?*

NOTE: If students have problems understanding this concept the phrase can be likened to Is this a problem for you? A demonstration may be required using simple, basic classroom ideas, e.g.,

*Would you mind if I borrowed your pencil?*
*Would you mind opening the window?*
*Would you mind sitting here?*
*Would you mind if I turned the air-conditioning off?*

2 If students are still struggling with the forms, keep the activity tightly controlled at first by eliciting answers and drilling: first chorally, then individually. Get two stronger students to demonstrate the first question before the rest of the class works in pairs. Check students are using the following with reasonable accuracy: pronunciation; appropriate forms of verbs with each phrase; appropriate responses to each request/offer.

**ANSWERS**

1  Would you mind if I used your phone?
2  Would your prefer tea or coffee?
3  Would you like me to call you a taxi?
4  Would you like to play golf next week?
5  Would you make me a copy of your new price list?
6  Would you mind giving me a lift to the airport?

## Starting and finishing calls

Finishing conversations is not easy! Students must be able to recognize and produce **Pre-closures** (preparing the listener for the end of the conversation) and **Closures** (ending the conversation).

In this activity we present/practise two pre-closures: *Anyway* and *Right, then*.

Point out that pre-closures are followed by a pause by the speaker. The person being spoken to will also use a pre-closure, such as *Fine*, to signal acceptance, or will recap.

A chart may help to explain this:

| Speaker 1 | Speaker 2 |
|---|---|
| Right, then. *(pause)* | |
| | Fine. I'll see you tomorrow, then. |
| Yes, see you. Bye. | |
| | Bye. |

14

**1** Remind students of the three conversations in the previous lessons and ask them to recall any phrases used to start or finish the calls. Refer students to the tapescripts if necessary. Students do the gap-fill individually. A rapid way to check their answers is to copy the chart onto an OHP with an overlay of the correct answers.

**ANSWERS**

Polite enquiries: *How are things?*
Saying why: *I'm phoning to ask...*
Ready to finish: *Anyway...*
Offering help: *Let me know if there's anything I can do.*
Future plans: *I'll look forward to seeing you on Tuesday, then.*
Ending: *Thank you for calling.*

**2** Explain that this exercise will check students can use the language from the previous activity in context.

Students do the exercise in pairs. Again, OHT is a speedy way to give feedback. You could also use negative checking by giving wrong phrases (e.g., *Have a nice day* at the beginning of the conversation) and encouraging students to correct.

**ANSWERS**

The Start
A *Nice to hear from you. How are you?*
B *How are things?*
B *I'm phoning to ask...*

The Finish
A *Give me a ring if you have any problems.* (or similar)
B *Right. See you...*
B *Thanks for your help.*
A *Have a nice day.*

## Telephone quiz

Telephone language is often highly colloquial in the students' own language as well as in English, so they often won't be able to translate directly the phrases they use in their own language.

Students do the quiz in groups if possible. During the feedback session, remember to score each group's answers as you go along.

**1 ANSWERS**

a I'll put you through.
b Hold on.
c It's engaged.

**2** Elicit examples rather than explanations for these phrases, e.g., the code for the students' home town or city, and get students to say which rooms in the building have extensions.

**3** If students are struggling, give paraphrases and ask students which sentences they refer to.

T *Can you hold on while I find the information?*
S *Can you bear with me a second?*

T *He's in a meeting at the moment.*
S *He's tied up at the moment.*

T *I can't hear you very well.*
S *You're very faint.*

T *I'll phone you again early in the morning.*
S *I'll get back to you first thing.*

T *Could you read out the information I've given to you so I can check it?*
S *Could you read that back to me?*

**4** This exercise is based on commonly made mistakes. Explain why the answers — though grammatically correct — are nevertheless inappropriate.

a *Who are you?* sounds aggressive.

b We often use *it is* or *this is*, rather than *I am*, when talking about names on the telephone.

c The polite response is *Sorry?* or *Could you repeat that please?* (in US English, *Excuse me?*).

d In a business context, when you don't know the person you're talking to, *No, she isn't* would sound impolite.

e *I don't care* implies a lack of interest and would therefore be impolite.

f *That's the lot* is colloquial English meaning 'that's all' or 'I've no more to add'.

*Yes, of course* is used when agreeing to a request.

15

## Making appointments

Freer practice:  Get four students to the front of the class to demonstrate the activity, then divide the class into groups of four. If possible, give each person a different coloured piece of paper to correspond with the coloured boxes in the activity, i.e., white, green, yellow, and blue. Then everyone will be sure which role each of them is to act out. Have a practice run — start the activity and prime as necessary.

**I**    Monitor during the activity but interrupt as little as possible and make notes on any mistakes (grammar, pronunciation, appropriateness) you notice. After a few minutes, get students to swap pieces of paper (and roles).

At the end, tell students how they have performed and mention mistakes you noted; provide further practice if necessary.

**2**    Books closed. Monitor as above. Students can still use their pieces of paper to swap roles. Feedback as above.

To give more opportunities for speaking, each of these activities can be done in pairs. This activity still works if teacher and student take it in turns to take three roles — with different voices!

## Pronunciation

**2**   🔲   Read the conversations to the students. (Tongue-twisters are difficult, even for native English speakers!  Make it fun and don't expect perfection.)

## Changing arrangements

**I**   If possible, write the lines of the conversation on separate strips of paper. Make enough for pairs or small groups (two to four students).

For one-to-one classes record the conversation and play it after the student has put sentences in the correct order.

If students get stuck or make mistakes, try to help them see the logical or functional connections between sentences.

Faster groups can practise in pairs, substituting their own ideas where possible. Provide feedback with model answer/recorded conversation.

**ANSWERS**
The correct order is:
4  II  IO  3  I  7  6  2  8  I2  9  5.

**2**   Remind students how phrasal verbs were used in conversation in 1 above. This should help them with deciding on meaning, whether a direct object is required or not, and the position of any direct object.

Do pairwork activity orally and drill some of the phrases chorally, then individually. Focus on the stress laid on the preposition in phrasal verbs,

e.g., *The meeting is off*.

**ANSWERS**
| | |
|---|---|
| I | Could we pencil it in? |
| 2 | I'm sorry to put you out. |
| 3 | I'm afraid the conference is off. |
| 4 | Something unexpected has come up. |
| 5 | We'll have to put off the meeting. |
| 6 | I can't pin them down. |
| 7 | I need to get in touch with my lawyer. |

# SKILLS WORK

## Listening

**I**   🔲   Students listen and do the activity, then check answers in pairs. If students have difficulty, go through with the whole class.

**ANSWERS**
The only thing not mentioned is stage lighting in the auditorium.

**2**   🔲   Students listen and do the activity. Check answers: one student answers, the others confirm or correct.

**ANSWERS**
| | |
|---|---|
| I | They don't know the numbers of delegates who wish to attend each talk. |
| 2 | Everyone — so IO7 delegates. |
| 3 | 9 o'clock — so they can get two sessions in before lunch. |

**4 A** find out the number of people going to each presentation and equipment needed;

**B** arrange sit-down meal.

## Speaking 1

Explain that this is an exercise in making precise arrangements; there *is* one perfect solution!

Divide the class into two groups.

Group One: (arranging conference): look at information on page 23 of Student's Book.

Group Two: (at Head Office): look at page 151.

Both groups should make sure they understand all the information and should start preparing things they may need to say.

After some minutes, divide students into pairs, made up of one student from each group. Student arranging conference phones student at Head Office to arrange the programme.

NOTE: Students might feel more comfortable doing this activity back-to-back to simulate the telephone situation more accurately. If resources permit, the best option is to use real telephones in different rooms.

## Speaking 2

**1** Explain that this is an exercise in making arrangements and that they can't do the activity without cancelling something.

Set up as in Speaking 1 above.

Group One: (at Headquarters): looks at information on page 23 of Student's Book.

Group Two: (UK Sales Director): looks at page 150.

At groupwork stage student takes one role, teacher takes second role. Give student time to prepare role, and assist as necessary.

**2** Explain to students that they have to change the arrangement they just made.

Set up by eliciting possible reasons for cancelling something, e.g., emergency board meeting, important customer, TV interview.

CLOSURE: Follow the procedure on page 11.

17

## PRESENTATION

> **Optional equipment and materials**
> OHT of table and pie chart on page 24
> OHT or handout of gapped sentences for
> exercise 4, page 25

Students look at the photos on page 24.

Ask students to name as many things as they can
and then ask them to give some words to link them
all. Possible answers for headwords include:
Cosmetics, Beauty Products, Women's Products.

**1** Ask students to read the instructions.

Elicit what they know about L'Oréal: students
should at least know that it is a cosmetics or
perfumery company.

**2** ▭ Check students understand the diagrams:

*What information does the pie chart give you?*
(Each division's share of total sales)

*What does 'turnover' mean?*

*Which activity has the biggest turnover?
Approximately how much of the company's
turnover is in perfumes and beauty?*

Check students understand the task: *What sort of
information are you going to listen for?*

Advise students not to write anything for the first
listening but try to get a global understanding.

Play the cassette once all the way through.

Play the cassette again, pausing after each relevant
section for each answer to give students time to
write in the information given. Students do the sums
to complete the table and pie chart. Students
compare answers in pairs.

Play the cassette again, without pausing.

Elicit correct answers. If possible, use an OHT of
the table and pie chart on the board; ask students to
write up answers and ask the class if they agree.

**ANSWERS**

| Turnover | FFr (bn) | % |
|---|---|---|
| Consumer and salons | 18.4 | 49.0 |
| Perfumes and beauty | 8.5 | 22.6 |
| Synthelabo | 6.3 | 16.8 |
| Active cosmetics | 3.7 | 9.8 |
| Other activities | 0.7 | 1.8 |
| Number of employees | 30,000+ | |
| Gross turnover | FFr 37.57bn | |

**3** ▭ Before students listen again, they can work in
pairs to try to fill in the gaps. Play the cassette,
pausing where relevant for the students to answer.
Students compare answers in pairs. Play again if
necessary. Ask students to find the tapescript on
page 162 and correct their answers. Play the cassette
once more while students follow the tapescript.

**ANSWERS**
1 facilities, agents, subsidiaries
2 revenue
3 range, brands
4 enhance, channel, distribution
5 advances, leader, field
6 hold, stake

**PX** If you can, bring in advertisements, brochures,
articles, etc. for several well-known companies for
students to look at and choose from. This will
enable pre-experience students to do this exercise.

**4** For weaker students, provide a list of gapped
sentences or cues, on either an OHT or a handout.

# LANGUAGE WORK

> **Optional equipment and materials**
>
> Word cards with numbers on for exercise 2, page 26
>
> Gapped sentences for exercise 3, page 27
>
> Handout of words for vocabulary activity, page 30

## Pronunciation

**1** 🔲 Introduce the lesson's topic by asking:

*What time is it?*
*What time is it in your country at the moment?* *
(for students studying in the UK)

*What time is it in Japan/USA/Britain/Europe, etc.?*
*What's your phone number?*
*When were you born?*
*How far is it from London to Paris by air?*
*What's the population of the UK?*
*What's the date today?*
*What time does this lesson finish?*
*How much did your watch/coat/jacket etc., cost?*

This can be done in pairs, but keep it short and snappy: it is a 'taster' only.

NOTE: If you substitute your own questions, don't pre-empt exercise 3.

Play section 1 of the cassette. Students write down, then compare answers. Play section 1 again. Do the same for the other sections. Wind cassette back to the beginning. Elicit correct answers verbally, then play relevant section again.

Allow students to read the tapescript on page 162 (while playing the cassette again if you wish).

**ANSWERS**

| | |
|---|---|
| 1 0865 267 622 | 6 1958, '59 |
| 2 16 | 7 8½ million or 8,500,000 |
| 3 60, ⅔ | 8 18.07, 18/7, 18th July, or 18 July |
| 4 1.6 | 9 16.50, 2.30; or 14.30 |
| 5 – 8° | 10 $999.99 |

NOTES on answers:
1 Make sure students heard and noted the pauses on the cassette in order to get the number groupings correct.

**2,3** Did students have 16 or 60? When numbers 13-19 are spoken in isolation the stress is *sixteen*. However, when they are part of a sentence, the stress moves: *He's sixteen years old*.

In numbers 20, 30, 40, etc., the stress is *sixty* and does not normally move.

For other answers, see Grammar and Usage notes in Student's Book, page 182.

**2** Allocate sections of the picture to each pair of students. One person from each pair reads out their numbers to the class. The other students say if they agree/disagree with the pronunciation. Practise with the whole class any numbers they had difficulty with. Put these numbers on word cards that you can 'flash' at students, or write some of them on the board, point and ask students to say the words.

**3** Write on the board numbers that are relevant to you. Ask students to guess what they are. Then explain the task. Monitor.

## Collecting information

**1** Ask students what they already know about AT&T. Explain that the aim of the activity is to collect more information about this company. Divide students into pairs, A and B.

Ask A students to look at the questions only; B students only look at the information about AT&T. A students ask B students about AT&T. Students close their books, recall the questions and practise them.

**2** Ask students how much they know about Robert Bosch GmbH and Komatsu. Do not confirm or correct their answers yet. Divide the class into groups A and B. Rearrange seating so that members of the same group can work together. A students look at the information on page 27 of their books. Group B students look at the information on page 152 in file 5 and prepare questions. Check that students understand all the vocabulary and have worked out the correct questions. Group A students now find a partner from Group B. In their pairs, students find out about their partner's company and make a note of the answers. Monitor. Students return to their groups and compare their answers.

Elicit correct answers and comment on students' performance. Students may now look at the other group's information.

NOTE: This information gap activity is relatively time-consuming to set up until students have done a few of them. However, it is well worth the time spent, since students practise speaking English in a realistic way, asking questions to which they do not know the answer. Bear in mind that the main aim is not really to find out the correct answers, but to improve students' language skills.

In one-to-one classes, teacher takes one of the roles and exchanges information with the student, ensuring that the student takes turns at asking and answering.

## Future predictions

**1** Ask students to make three predictions about business in the future in the fields of: money; working from home; hours of work.

Read the introduction and the four questions with the students. Check students understand *hierarchical, unemployment, prejudice*. Students do not need to understand every word. After two minutes, elicit answers, explaining why they are correct or incorrect.

**ANSWERS**

| 1 | Peter Vestergaard Larsen | 3 | Richard Dantas |
|---|---|---|---|
| 2 | Vivek Sood | 4 | Ted Ochs |

**2** Explain the task and do the first answer with the students as an example.

Ask students to say the words after you for correct pronunciation.

**ANSWERS**

| 1 | dec<u>li</u>ning | 3 | <u>comm</u>onplace |
|---|---|---|---|
| 2 | <u>sca</u>rce | 4 | <u>par</u>t-<u>ti</u>me |

**3** These difficult concepts may need further explanation.

**ANSWERS**
1 Who's Who
2 minorities
3 the glass ceiling
4 an array
5 rightful

**4** Check/teach the meaning of each noun. Ask students to guess what the adjectives are before they look back at the text for answers.

Students say the words after you; point out that the stress 'moves' on some adjectives (see answers).

**ANSWERS**

| bur<u>eau</u>cracy | bureau<u>cra</u>tic |
|---|---|
| entrepr<u>eneur</u> | entrepr<u>eneu</u>rial |
| flexib<u>ili</u>ty | <u>flex</u>ible |
| cre<u>a</u>tion | cre<u>a</u>tive |

**5** Ask students to complete the exercise without looking at the text. After two minutes for the task, ask students to self-correct from the text.

Check students understand all the phrases.

**ANSWERS**
1 c   2 f   3 e   4 a   5 d   6 b

**6** Refer students to Vivek Sood's prediction and ask them to underline the verbs.

Elicit answers *will make* and *will become* and explain that these are used to talk about the future.

Students look at the sample dialogue in 6. Practise it: ask them to repeat the sentences after you, then ask two different pairs of students to demonstrate it to the rest of the class.

Highlight and practise the contractions of *will* in *there'll* (pronounced /ðeəl/) and *it'll* (pronounced /ɪtl/). Elicit the contractions for the other forms (*I, you, he*, etc.) Elicit other possible questions students could ask and practise them, e.g.,

*Do you think there'll be more women managers?*
*Do you agree that police forces will be privatized?*

Monitor while students work in pairs, then give feedback. Ask any pairs who had particularly good ideas to repeat their dialogues for the class.

**7** Elicit some ideas about each issue, in a class or group discussion.

Elicit/teach some phrases useful to express ideas in writing (adapt/select according to the level of the class):

*I believe there will be ...*
*I disagree with the idea that ...*
*It will be good if ...*
*It will be a disaster if ...*
*I hope ...*

20

Students complete the written work in class or for homework. Collect in work for correction, or encourage students to 'swap' and correct each others'.

NOTE: Ask students to bring a notebook to the next lesson for new vocabulary.

# RECORDING VOCABULARY

Revise the vocabulary covered in the previous lesson. To revise spelling, give the words as anagrams on the board or on a handout. To revise meanings, ask questions beginning *What's the opposite of ...?*; *What's the word that means ...?*; *What's the adjective of ...?*

Ask students the questions in Exercise 1. Ask *Is it better to store words alphabetically or in groups?* Point out that alphabetical order makes the words easier to find, but that grouping words makes them easier to remember. So, store each new word twice.

Show students how to make a vocabulary notebook:

- Leave the first three pages blank to build up an index of topics.

- Use the last 26 pages as an alphabetical list.

- Use the remaining pages to record vocabulary under topic headings.

- As new words go in, write any new topic headings on first three pages.

- Ask students for topic headings based on work covered so far.

Work through the other ideas on recording vocabulary and mention the advantages of each and the importance of regularly testing yourself; using:

- notebook: use two columns on each page so one can be covered or folded.

- cards: word one side, meaning the other. Good for testing yourself.

- computer: you can revise in your lunch hour or in spare moments at work.

# SKILLS WORK

> **Equipment and materials**
> Students need a pencil, ruler, eraser, and possibly a pair of compasses.
> Large sheets of paper would be useful.
> Alternatively, students could draw their diagrams on to OHTs.

## Speaking

1 You ask, or students ask each other:

*What is a diagram?*
*What do we use them for?*
*What headings would you expect to find in a diagram on company structure?*

Check students understand *formulate policy*. Students ask each other the questions in 1 in pairs. Elicit answers, checking pronunciation. Rest of the exercise as for 1 above.

**ANSWERS**

| 1 | shareholders | 4 | customers |
|---|---|---|---|
| 2 | suppliers | 5 | staff |
| 3 | board of directors | | |

2 Check students understand all the vocabulary in the questions, e.g., *deals with*, *records transactions*, *schedules* (verb), *monitors*, etc.

Point out that the present simple tense has been used and ask why.

SUPPLEMENTARY ACTIVITY: Ask students to remember/revise the questions by using the answers as prompts. Practise/drill any that students find difficult, e.g.,
T *What was the question we used for production?*
S *What part of the organization manufactures the products?*

**ANSWERS**
1 production
2 marketing and sales
3 human resources
4 research and development
5 purchasing
6 distribution
7 finance and administration
8 management and control

**3** Students discuss the three questions in pairs.

Students draw a diagram of their own organization using the materials mentioned above. They should not let anyone else see it at this stage. Remind students of the grammar and vocabulary to use. Ideally, give them two or three minutes to prepare what they want to say.

In pairs or groups, students describe their organization; the others listen and try to sketch a diagram of its according to what the student says. Student compare the original diagram with the sketch, and discuss any 'mistakes' or differences. Monitor during the activity and give feedback afterwards. The diagrams could be displayed on the classroom walls.

**PX** As an alternative, pre-experience students could use information about a well-known or imaginary company or use the structure of their college or language school.

## Reading

**1** Ask students to keep their books closed. Find out how much they know about Microsoft but do not confirm or correct at this stage or give further information.

Write the following headings on the board. Explain that each is for a different paragraph of an article about Microsoft. Elicit what the headings mean, and encourage students to predict what each paragraph will say.

| | |
|---|---|
| hard work | frugal |
| competitive | tough |
| challenging | fun |

**2** Students check their predictions by reading the article and decide whether they would like to work for Microsoft . Elicit responses from one or two students.

**3** In a one-to-one situation, or with less advanced classes, it might be better to provide answers to which students must devise appropriate questions:

1  Over $3 billion.
   (*What are Microsoft's annual sales?*)

2  One reason is because it saves money.
   (*Why do they understaff their product teams?*)

3  Bill Gates.
   (*Who is the Chief Executive Officer?*)

4  Because they keep fighting and they never give up.
   (*Why are they more competitive?*)

5  Because their bosses often criticize them.
   (*Why do their employees have to stand up for themselves?*)

6  By giving them responsibility straight away.
   (*How do they make the work more challenging?*)

7  Individuality.
   (*What do they encourage?*)

**4** Ask students to write the answers to the exercise, then to compare answers in pairs.

Elicit correct answers checking pronunciation as you do so.

Remind students to add new words to their vocabulary notebooks.

**ANSWERS**
overcharge/undercharge
overweight/underweight
underpaid
oversleep
overdrawn

Other common phrases students might suggest are: *overtired, overexcited, overeat, overheat, overcook, overexpand, undercook, underutilize*, etc.

**5** Students can discuss the questions in pairs.

**6** Students could work on this as a presentation to the rest of the class. Give them a few minutes to prepare/make notes. Make notes during the presentation and ask the rest of the class to think of supplementary questions for the end.

**PX** As an alternative, pre-experience students could prepare a presentation on the kind of company they would prefer to work for.

CLOSURE: Follow the procedure on page 11.

# PRESENTATION

Ask students when people need to give presentations and what aids they need to help them.

**1** ⬛ Let students look closely at the photographs before listening, but don't confirm or correct the vocabulary since it is part of the listening test.

**ANSWERS**
Fax of map (i); overhead projector (h); display stand (b)

**2** Play the tape again if necessary, stopping at the critical points.

**ANSWERS**
Bob is going to do: 1 2 4 7
Victoire is going to do: 3 5 6 8

**3** ⬛

**ANSWERS**
1 Should, don't, should
2 Aren't you going to, I'll, shall, will, leave

KEY LANGUAGE POINTS:

1 Note that negation often moves from the main verb to the introductory verb in sentences like

*I think we shouldn't — I don't think we should*

2 *Bring* means 'to where I am, or will be in the future'

*Bring the notes here.*
*Bring the notes to the meeting tomorrow.*

*Take* means 'to another place'

*Take the notes to Jim.*
*Take the notes to the meeting — I won't be there.*

**4** **ANSWERS**
1 Checking everything again — Bob implied it wasn't necessary.
2 Bob not reading the notes — Victoire thought he should have read them already.
3 Victoire leaving the meeting — Bob thought both of them should be there.

**5** Get students with interesting ideas to tell the rest of the class.

# LANGUAGE WORK

**Optional equipment and materials**

Role play cards and action plan for exercise 1, page 39

Dictionaries for exercise 2, page 40

## International meetings

**1** Let students read the introduction, then check comprehension with a series of quick questions:

*How long is the conference? Where is it?* etc.

Give students time to answer the questions — tell them to underline vocabulary they can't work out.

Deal with vocabulary difficulties, using other students to explain as far as possible.

**2** Remind students that these are now plans, so you need to use *going to*.

Tell students about interesting ideas you hear during monitoring.

**3** Tell students:

*At the conference there are German, Dutch, Italian and North American managers. Will the actions you have decided on offend any of them? Read what this consultant says about the culture of meetings.*

Elicit responses from students, e.g.,

Teacher: *What are you going to do, Pierre?*
  Pierre: *I'm going to have a quick look at the papers.*
Teacher: *Will that offend anyone?*
  Pierre: *The Germans and the Dutch, but not the Italians.*

Check vocabulary by asking students what they remember about each heading, e.g., **Sending a subordinate**:

*British people do it but Spanish don't.*

## Asking for opinions

**I** Show how the same opinion can be expressed in a number of ways:

1  *There should be ... * + noun phrase
2  *We should have ... * + noun phrase
3  *They should ... * + verb phrase
4  noun + *should be* + past participle (passive form of 3)

Practise with a few phrases from exercise 3.

NOTE: some phrases work better with one structure than with others.

**2** Practise with replies which reflect the structure of the question:

1  Should there...?    There should.
2  Should we...?    We should.
3  Should they...?    They should.
4  Should it be...?    It should.

**3** You may need to elicit why some of these are 'green' issues:

1  Public transport:    fewer emissions
2  Unleaded petrol:    less damage to air quality
5  Nuclear fuel:        problem of waste disposal

Monitor and get students to repeat good arguments for the whole class.

NOTE: You might like to point out that some of these issues are contentious and students should be aware that what is general opinion in one culture may be quite unacceptable in another.

## Managing the Environment

PX  With pre-experience classes, give the students roles — Managing Director, Financial Director, Marketing Director — and some idea of these people's main concerns.  Discuss and practise some 'meetings vocabulary' and the role of the chairman in conducting the contributions of others.  Then continue as follows:

**I** Make sure the instructions are clear by comprehension checks:

1  *Who are you?*
2  *What are you concerned about?*
3  *How did you get the proposals?*
4  *What are the three things you can do with each proposal — in your own words?*
5  *What must you do if you decide to go ahead with a proposal — there are three things.*

Don't worry about explaining the individual proposals as the groups should be able to work them out, but be prepared to assist during monitoring.

PX  With a group which is not particularly well organized, or with pre-experience students, you can give an action plan (on a handout or OHT):

| Proposal | Plan of action | Person responsible | Resources allocated |
|---|---|---|---|
|  |  |  |  |

**2** Students use the summary above or their own notes.

**3** Follow procedure in the Student's Book.

As a supplementary activity, see if students can remember what the suggestions were which contained these verbs:

1  take away          (company cars)
2  install            (solar cells/fan)
3  ban                (office memos)
4  collect and recycle  (waste paper)
5  sell               (vegetarian food)
6  contribute         (to the Green Party)
7  change             (light bulbs)
8  plant              (trees)
9  scrap              (lorries)

Work backwards from the answers to see if students can remember the accompanying verbs. Get students to explain once again how each suggestion might help in managing the environment.

## Pronunciation

1 ▭ If necessary, exaggerate the difference in length since students who are struggling with this will reduce the length when they imitate. Point out the phonemic transcription used in English/English dictionaries, and explain that : is a length marker. This should enable students to use a dictionary to check their answers to exercise 2.

2 Students use an English/English dictionary with phonemic transcription to check their ideas.

**ANSWERS**
/ɪ/ — list, fill, slip, live
/iː/ — least, feel, sleep, leave

The following order emerges, with possible action suggested. (Other orders are possible but students would need to justify them):

1 Telephone message — dissatisfied customer — call and sort it out.
2 Cherwell Catering — menus — unsatisfactory due to inclusion of pork on both — call and sort it out.
3 Fax from Gold Shield — hotel booking for agent — First the students may decide to do it — but after reading the Telex (**8**), they should contact Gold Shield and explain Claire Patterson will no longer be available on the 15th.
4 Internal memo — budget meeting — send memo with regrets.
5 Letter — cancelled order — send memo to despatch department.
6 Note — re brochures — send memo asking them to hold them until Claire's return on Monday 19th if possible.
7 Letter — sales seminar — send letter with regrets.
8 Telex — re delayed return — arrange for someone to pick her up — contact Gold Shield Securities (see **3** above).

# SKILLS WORK

## Speaking

It is probably a good idea to give a time limit for this 'Team work' activity, to try to ensure that students skim the documents rather than reading them word for word.

(The exercise took a native speaker experienced in prioritizing correspondence 10 minutes.)

2 This should give rise to a fair amount of discussion and disagreement. You might like to deal with the question of important = 'important to the company and the departmental objectives'.

**POSSIBLE ANSWER**
On the basis of the following priorities
(most important first)
A things to do with customers
B things to do with agents
C urgent internal matters
D things to do with suppliers
E routine internal matters

## Writing

1 After students have considered, refer them to the Grammar and Usage notes on page 186 to check their ideas. Use the board to highlight key differences between the three documents.

2 In the feedback, write a list on the board which students can copy down.

Check production of the abbreviations by working backwards from the meanings and getting students to say or write the abbreviations.

**ANSWERS**

*Letters*
encs   Enclosures: things that are included in the envelope
pp   Per pro: signed on behalf of someone else
c.c.   carbon copy: Who else you are sending this to
re   Regarding: what the letter is about
attn   Attention: who the letter is for

*Fax*
dept   division or department
attn   Attention: who the fax is for

25

*Telex*

| tnks | Thanks |
|------|--------|
| pls | Please |
| tlx | Telex |
| rgds | Regards |
| attn | Attention |
| asap | As soon as possible |
| pdq | Pretty damn quick — a slang version of asap |

**3**  ANSWERS

| Refer: | *Thank you for your ..., Further to our ..., With reference to ...* |
|--------|-----------------------------------------------------------------|
| Good news: | *You will be pleased to hear ..., I am delighted to tell you ...* |
| Bad news: | *I regret to inform you ..., Unfortunately ...* |
| Offer help: | *If we can be of further assistance ..., I would be happy to ..., Would you like me to ...* |
| Make requests: | *Could you possibly ..., We would be grateful if you could ..., I'd appreciate it if you could ..., Pls ...* |
| Apologize: | *I am sorry about ..., I am sorry for any inconvenience caused ...* |
| Refer to future contact: | *I will of, course, contact you again ..., Let us know ...by ..., Please do not hesitate to ..., Looking forward to ...* |

**4**  This leads on from the last activity but it might be better to come back to it at a later date, when students have begun to forget the in-tray exercise.

ANSWERS

enquire
Further to ...
You will be pleased to hear that ...
I am afraid ...
Could you possibly ...?
Would you like me to ...?
... any inconvenience caused.
Please find enclosed ...
... please do not hesitate to ask.
... seeing you on the 29th.

**5**  Get students to find pairs of formal/informal statements and requests using the completed table in activity 4.

ANSWERS

| Formal | Informal |
|--------|----------|
| With reference to | Thank you for |
| I am delighted to tell you | You will be pleased to hear |
| We regret to inform you | I am afraid |
| I would appreciate it if you could | Could you possibly |
| If you wish, we would be happy to | Would you like me to |
| Please find enclosed | I am enclosing |
| I look forward to | Looking forward to |

**6**  First establish whether fax or letter is better (this will also serve to check comprehension). Then do the first two opening and closing phrases on the board as examples. Monitor and offer corrections/improvements during written work.

ANSWERS

| I | Fax | speed is important, matter is not confidential |
|---|-----|------------------------------------------------|
| 2 | Letter | fax would be expensive and the matter is not urgent |
| 3 | Fax or letter | it depends how urgent you think it is |
| 4 | Fax | contacts with customers are always urgent |
| 5 | Letter | more personal in this case |
| 6 | Fax | it is now urgent since you forgot to do it |
| 7 | Fax | since it's urgent, but letter if it is very long |

**7**  Get students to pick from exercise 6 the one which is closest to the type of letters or faxes they really have to send.

PX  For pre-experience students, pick the one which you think is closest to their needs.

CLOSURE:  Follow the procedure on page 11.

# 5 Growth and Development

## PRESENTATION

**1** General discussion

**PX** ALTERNATIVE PRESENTATION: (Just in case you have students who are completely unfamiliar with computers.)
Elicit/teach the following:

In computing we need *hardware* and *software*.

*Hardware* is the actual equipment such as the *keyboard, mouse, monitor, disk drive, printer,* and *modem*.

There are two types of *software*:

1   *Programs* — like the *disk operating system* or *DOS* — which tell the computer how to read the disk and run the printer.

2   Programs which perform particular tasks like *word processing, database management, spreadsheets*. These are called *applications* or *packages*.

*Software programs* may be on the *hard disk*, on *floppy disks*, or even inside the computer in ROM (Read-Only Memory).

PCs, or *Personal Computers*, are an important part of the market because they can be joined together or *networked*. Very large companies still use *mini-computers*, which are much bigger.

**2** 🔲 Ask students to read the introduction then check comprehension.

Who are they going to hear?
*A manager of SOFTBANK.*

What is he talking about?
*The growth and development of the company.*

Why is the company important in Japan?
*It distributes half the PC software sold in Japan.*

Students read activity 1. Talk about what the three product areas mean. With a less advanced group, you could play the first part of the tape now. Otherwise students look at activity 2 and think what order might be logical, then play the tape. Check answers. If students have struggled, play the tape again and highlight the key points.

**ANSWERS**
1   Games, business applications, networking (Because he starts by talking about *now* and then talks about *before that* and *before that*)

2   The correct order, with notes, is:
    1   They set up the distribution business.
    2   They set up the publishing division.
        (*... just six months after we'd set up ...*)
    3   They launched two magazines.
    4   The magazines didn't sell.
        (*... 85% were returned ... they just didn't sell ...*)
    5   They decided to take a gamble.
    6   They changed the layout of the magazines.
    7   They advertised the magazines on TV.
        (*... spent all the money we had left on TV advertising ...*)
    8   The magazines sold out in three days.

**3** ANSWERS 🔲
1   Since 1981
2   Operating systems, cables, boards
3   14 different ones
4   1981 or 1982
5   They didn't want people to think they were in trouble.

**4** Remind less advanced students of the different tenses they have studied and get examples on the board.

**ANSWERS**
1   has been distributing
2   were distributing
3   had been distributing
4   distributed

# LANGUAGE WORK

┌─────────────────────────────────────────────┐
**Optional equipment and materials**
Photocopies, cut up, of stories and endings,
page 52
└─────────────────────────────────────────────┘

## A career

**1** This activity reinforces the use of the simple past for narrative. It also encourages students to interact with the text by forcing them to make predictions before moving on. Finally the form of the activity means that students are encouraged to skip around, useful practice in the technique of scanning.

If your students might know who Robert Maxwell was, tell them the story is about a man who became famous under a different name. Ask them to guess after each piece of information who it is.

**2** Sudents go back to the text to find information and relate it to other pieces of information — another skill in scanning.

**ANSWER**
7  5  3  9  4  8  1  6  2

**3** As in Student's Book.

**4** Tell students they do not need to know all the expressions to identify which verb goes with each group.

**ANSWERS**
1 c  2 f  3 a  4 e  5 h  6 b  7 g  8 d

## Finding things in common

These questions work well if you can put students in groups with people from the same country, city or even company. In a multi-lingual, multi-cultural class be prepared to offer topics such as:

countries they have visited
languages they speak
family
pets
subjects they studied at school
things they like and dislike

**PX** Explain to pre-experience students that finding things in common with customers and clients is an important skill since it helps to put the business relationship on a more personal basis. Then continue with normal presentation.

KEY LANGUAGE POINT: When students find things in common they will need to use *both* or *neither*. Supply them with at least the basic structures:

| We | | both | like/d.... |
|---|---|---|---|
| | are | both | studying... |
| | are | both | going to go... |
| | have | both | visited... |
| Neither of us | | | like/d.... |
| | is | | (studying).... |
| | is | | going to go... |
| | has | | visited.... |

## Past experiences

**1** Ask students to read the introduction and then check with comprehension questions or, as a change, a 'Many a Slip' game: Ask students to cover the introduction while you read it again with mistakes. Do not stop unless students shout out. Then stop, ask the students to correct, and continue:

*Masayoshi Daughter died in Kyushu, China in 1975. She is the founder of SOFTWARE, Japan's leading PC hardware distributor. Read his account of how he came to close the business and work out how long his hair is.*

**ANSWERS**
The answer could be: from the age of 16 when he went to the States, or since he came back from the States, or since 1979.

**2** This activity establishes the landmarks in the narrative, all of which are given by using the past tense. Activity 3 contrasts this with events started in the past and still happening.

Deal with any difficulties by highlighting the part of the text which gives the answer:

28

*I was living in Kyushu at the time. It was 1979 and I'd just come back from the States ... I'd gone to the States to study when I was 16 (1957+16=1973) ... I went to Oakland, California for a couple of years first, then transferred to Berkeley ... so in 1981 we finally moved to Tokyo...*

**ANSWERS**

| 1957 | 1973 | 1975 | 1979 | 1981 |
|------|------|------|------|------|
| Kyushu | Oakland | Berkeley | Kyushu | Tokyo |

**3** Let students try the activity but be prepared to stop them and re-teach the ideas concerning past and present perfect if necessary.

**ANSWERS**

1 How long did he stay? — two years
2 How long has he lived/been living? — since 1981
3 How long was he unemployed? — two years
4 How long has he run/been running? — since 1981
5 How long did he study? — four years
6 How long did he spend? — eight years
7 How long has he had? — since 1981

**4** **PX** With pre-experience students, substitute the following for 1–3:

1 Where do you study at the moment?
2 How long have you studied there?
3 Where did you study before that?

SUPPLEMENTARY ACTIVITIES:

1 Make sure students can use the main 'life event' verbs:

| | |
|---|---|
| started | gave up |
| left | resigned/was dismissed |
| joined | had (a child) |
| got (a job/married) | bought |
| moved | sold |
| began | visited |
| passed/failed | stayed |

2 Ask students to describe the career of one or both of their parents.

## Travellers' stories

**1** You could photocopy the stories and endings, give them out separately and ask students with the stories to find a person with a suitable ending.

For an alternative procedure, ask students to cover the endings, A–D, and take plenty of time to read the stories and think how they might end. Perhaps test their comprehension by suggesting some endings. Then ask them to find the correct ending.

**ANSWERS**
1 c  2 a  3 b  4 d

**2** **ANSWERS**
Scene setting — past continuous
Main events — simple past

**3** **ANSWERS**
The moment when he felt worried is the key focus of the story. Events at this time are told in the simple past. Everything before is in the past perfect.

**4** **ANSWERS**
*Story 3*  Past perfect — *had gone*
           Past continuous — *was working*
*Story 4*  Past perfect — *had packed, had done*
           Past continuous — *was watching*

Past perfect for events before the time of the narrative focus.

Past continuous for setting the scene of the narrative.

**5** It might help if students draw a time line of events and then fix the narrative focus. You can help them to use the correct tenses:

Past perfect for events before the narrative focus

Past continuous for events around the narrative focus

Simple past for the events of the story.

This activity can be set at the end of one lesson for telling at the beginning of the next.

Suggest that if students are having difficulty thinking of true stories, they can invent one and later the other students can guess whether their story was true or not.

# SKILLS WORK

| Optional equipment and materials |
| --- |
| LEGO bricks for exercise 1, page 53 |

## Speaking

Give students time to read up to *Tell a colleague about it*. Try to elicit the three parts of the narrative and draw them on the board on a time line, e.g., *Last year we changed the system ...*

| Before the change | The change | After the change |
| --- | --- | --- |
| The old system | The new system | The results |

Try to elicit the tenses which go with the time references, if we are focusing on the change:

| *Before ...* | *Then ...* | *Afterwards ...* |
| --- | --- | --- |
| We did this | Last year we changed to this | These things happened as a result |

Students make notes, then put students in pairs for the narrative. Monitor, and if you hear a particularly good narrative, ask the student to repeat it to the rest of the class.

## Listening

1  It doesn't matter if the students know nothing but having some LEGO bricks would be nice!

2  ▭  Ask quick comprehension questions:

1  What is the vertical scale? — Number of employees

2  What is the horizontal scale? — Time in years

3  What does the graph represent? — The growth of LEGO between 1932 and 1958.

4  Does anything on the graph surprise you? — (e.g., the increase in number of employees after fire destroyed the factory; the fact that the company was founded in 1932; the rapid increase in number of employees during the war and shortly after; the fact that plastic products were made in 1947)

Check students' comprehension of the task and perhaps do the first listening extract as an example. Pause after each extract while students digest the information and decide which part of the graph is referred to. If students are struggling, play sections again, pausing after key words and phrases.

**ANSWERS**

| 1 | 1949 | First building bricks |
| --- | --- | --- |
| 2 | 1932 | Company founded |
| 3 | 1958 | Ole Kirk succeeded by Godtfred Kirk. |
| 4 | 1955 | LEGO system of play launched. |
| 5 | 1942 | Fire destroyed the factory. |
| 6 | 1956 | First foreign sales company established in Germany. |
| 7 | 1934 | Adopted the name of LEGO. |
| 8 | 1947 | Equipment purchased to produce plastics. |

3  ▭

NOTE: Let students read the question then play the extract. Play all eight extracts to keep the focus on listening, then check the answers.

**ANSWERS**

1  Sale or return
2  Wooden toys
3  12
4  They could be part of a play system.
5  It was underinsured
6  The man who introduced LEGO products to the German market.
7  The Danish for 'play well', although it also means 'I assemble' in Latin.
8  They will never take the place of wood!

SUPPLEMENTARY ACTIVITY: Ask students if they can remember what these expressions applied to.

*In the story of the growth and development of LEGO what or who...*

1  were not very successful *(the first LEGO bricks)*
2  were left over *(little bits of wood)*
3  was the natural person *(Ole Kirk's son)*
4  had potential *(the LEGO bricks)*
5  was a disaster *(the fire)*
6  was attracted (to the idea of LEGO) *(Axel Thomsen)*
7  was a prize-winner *(Ole himself)*
8  was totally wrong *(the Danish toy trade magazine article)*

Reverse the activity and get students to say something about each answer, e.g.,

1   *The first LEGO bricks ... were not very successful.*

As a bridge to the next activity, ask students what they think the significant events in the history of LEGO are, e.g., *The meeting with a toy buyer was a turning point.*

**4**   As in Student's Book

## Pronunciation

**5**   [cassette]   Give students a few moments to work out the rules, then ask them to predict what the endings will sound like.  Play the tape to confirm or correct their ideas.  Then get the students to make the rules explicit.

**ANSWERS**

| /d/ | /t/ | /ɪd/ |
|---|---|---|
| destroyed | purchased | founded |
| manufactured | launched | adopted |
| died | established | succeeded |

The rules for regular past tense endings are:

1   Verbs ending in a voiced consonant or vowel, add /d/
2   Verbs ending in an unvoiced consonant, add /t/

   *Except*
3   Verbs endings in /d/ or /t/, add /ɪd/

Supplementary activity: Do a quick check on the meaning of the words listed above, e.g., *Who founded what?*

CLOSURE: Follow the procedure on page 11.

# **6** Problem Solving

---

| | |
|---|---|
| **Optional equipment and materials** | |
| Handout of blank chart for exercise 2, page 56 | |

## PRESENTATION

Explain that this unit is about solving problems and making decisions.

Remind students of (or in the case of pre-experience students, introduce them to) the stages of problem solving and decision making.

Define problem                     *What*

Set criteria for
solution                           *How much, how long,* etc.

Generate alternatives              *This, or this, or this?*

Evaluate alternatives              *Quicker, cheaper,* etc.

Choose                             *This is best, because...*

Inform                             Finance Department,
                                   Personnel, etc.

**PX** With a weak group or with pre-experience students work through a simple example, e.g.,

Going on a journey:

*Where do we want to go?*
*How much can we spend? How long can we take?*
*What are the possible ways?*
*Which is the best way?*
*So what's the decision?*
*Who have we got to tell?*

**1** Elicit possible answers but don't confirm or correct. Deal with any vocabulary that is not explained in the tapescripts in 2.

**2** ANSWERS 📼

*Anticlockwise from top left-hand picture*
**a** (Man and woman discussing schedule chart)
   Conversation 4

**b** (Man showing woman faulty motor)
   Conversation 3
**c** (Man and woman at airport)
   Conversation 1
**d** (Woman examining component, man calculating)
   Conversation 5
**e** (Man and woman studing an invoice)
   Conversation 2

If possible give out blank charts for students to fill in answers. Then ask class for answers to complete the chart on the board.

| Problem | Criteria | Alternatives | Decision |
|---|---|---|---|
| 1 travel to the centre | comfort, not expense | metro/taxi | taxi |
| 2 under-charge on invoice | paid? | call them/ do nothing | call them |
| 3 motor not working | keep within guarantee, cost of call out | take the back off/ call the engineer/ find out call-out fee | find out call-out fee |
| 4 behind schedule | make up time, keep costs down | overtime/ re-schedule | re-schedule |
| 5 price too high | price, potential sales | buy 30/ buy 100 | buy 30 |

**3** 📼 Before playing each extract give students time to guess what the missing words might be (one word per dotted line). Elicit ideas, but don't confirm or correct.

Grammar is dealt with in LANGUAGE WORK section.

**ANSWERS**
**1** How about taking, why don't we take
**2** Paid this, we'd better
**3** Could, the answer, charge
**4** I think we should, simply not feasible
**5** We buy, will they give us, we bought

**4** Students work individually, then check answers in pairs. If dictionaries are available, students use them to check.

**ANSWERS**

| | | | |
|---|---|---|---|
| 1 | tip | 5 | fare |
| 2 | commission | 6 | wages |
| 3 | charge | 7 | salary |
| 4 | fees | | |

Do a negative check by saying wrong sentences and getting students to correct:

*I gave the taxi driver commission.*
*The doctor's charge was very high.*
*Every month he gets $2000 in wages.*
*The fee to London is £24.*
*We offer our agents 15% tip.*

**5** **ANSWERS**

1 fare; tip
2 charge
3 wages
4 salary, commission
5 fees

# LANGUAGE WORK

---
**Equipment and materials**

handout of blank chart (same as for
PRESENTATION section)

---

## Making suggestions

**1** Before starting the exercise, remind students of ways of making suggestions which they heard in the last lesson. If possible elicit all the exponents from the students. Get the phrases on the board.

Students will find it more interesting to work in groups.

Go through the answers, including the reasons for the answers.

**ANSWERS**

Most forceful: *we'd better* — it is as if the decision had been made already

Least forceful: *we could* — not even the speaker is sure

*How about* + gerund — prepositions are always followed by the gerund form of verbs

*'d* in *We'd better* = *had* — the derivation of this colloquialism is obscure; *it would be better if we* is far easier to understand

*I don't think we should* — negation moves onto introductory verb

*We'd better not* — a set phrase.

**2** Check that students understand the task by asking them to explain it in their own words. Perhaps find the most enthusiastic phrase together. When they have got the answers, practise pitch range and intonation, through choral and individual repetition.

**ANSWERS**

1 That's a good idea.
2 That might be the answer.
3 I'm not sure about that.
4 I don't think we should.
5 No, that's simply not feasible.

**3** Revise stages of problem solving and decision making and if possible, give out blank charts for pairs to fill in (see Presentation, exercise 2 above). Work through the first problem.

Also remind students to use a range of suggestion expressions. Monitor and guide if feasible. End by bringing together the best solutions to each problem.

| Problem | Criteria | Alternatives | Decision |
|---|---|---|---|
| 1 find new product | sells in summer? connected with current products? | water skis grass skis roller skates skateboards | water skis |

## Considering possibilities

**1** ANSWERS

 1  *Will, would*

 2  *If* + present, future simple, *if* + past, *would* + infinitive

 3  *If* + present suggests B thinks it's quite likely (of course, since A says s/he will!).

 *If* + past suggests s/he thinks it is unlikely (again, responding to A's choice of structure. *What if ..?*)

**2** Emphasize that two students then try a few examples to make sure they have got the idea, e.g., *Head-hunter — I don't think that's likely.*

**3** Work through two examples carefully. Get students to explain what they must do in their own words before going on to the sentence-making activity.

Double check the concept and the grammar, e.g.,

*What do we use with **present**? That's right, **future**. So you think this is quite likely, do you?*

## Pronunciation

**1**  ▭  Do not stop the tape but play the whole thing again if students are struggling.

ANSWERS
 1  offers, I'll refuse
 2  continues, we'll all be
 3  moved, it'd be
 4  arrive, they'll be
 5  increased, we'd have to
 6  made, I'd start

**2** Although these sounds *are* important, make sure that students don't over-emphasize them when repeating the sentences.

## A shrinkage problem

**1** Check comprehension, perhaps with a 'Many a Slip' game (see page 28).

*You walk a chain of small newspaper shops. You have a decreasing number of solutions with wastage: that is, loss of staff through theft. Members of staff suspect you are as much to blame as the staff.*

Double check:

shrinkage     jargon meaning loss of stock, largely due to theft by staff and/or customers

*newsagent's*    a shop which sells newspapers, confectionery, tobacco

Ask students what they should do with the proposals.

Go through examples and check why the speaker has changed the tense. Conduct as a teacher-centred activity this is a good preparation for activities 2 and 3 below. Give students time to read each proposal and think about a) their reaction (use 1st or 2nd conditional?) and b) the consequences.

**2** As in Student's Book

**3** Remind students of the structure of meetings. If necessary appoint a chairman.

SUPPLEMENTARY ACTIVITY: Revise nouns from this lesson by asking:

*What words can you remember from this lesson which are connected with **shops**?* (tills, exits, uniforms, electronic tags, labels, alarms, discounts, stock, customers)

*Control* and *check*: Let students read the note and explain the difference in their own words.

**4** General discussion

 PX  With pre-experience students, change the question from *work place* to *school or college* and from *How did you deal with them?* to *How did the authorities deal with them?*

34

## Negotiating solutions

1 Work through the example conversation, highlighting the grammatical structures and linking them to the meaning conveyed, i.e.,

1st conditional = speaker thinks it's likely
2nd conditional = speaker thinks it's unlikely

so the structure of the conversations is:

A likely suggestion
B agreement
A unlikely suggestion
B refusal

Deal with the structure of acceptance and refusal.

Build up conversation 1 with students. Then let students do 2, 3, and 4.

2 Explain that a different structure from that in 1 above is possible in negotiations.

Problem
A suggestion
B refusal
A modified suggestion 1
B limited agreement
A modified suggestion 2
B agreement

Point out that the modified suggestion 2 is not what A really wanted and the agreement from B is not what they really wanted. It is a compromise.

Work through problem 1 together putting language on to the ideas, e.g.,

Financial Manager: We must stop sending gifts to customers at Christmas. It's too expensive.

Sales Manager: I can't agree to that. The gifts are an important part of our image advertising.

Financial Manager: Well, I think we should stopping sending the whisky at least.

Sales Manager: I agree to some extent. If we sent diaries and calendars to our small suppliers and a bottle of whisky to our larger customers rather than a case, that would save a lot of money.

Financial Manager: What about only sending a bottle of whisky to customers who do more than $50,000 worth of business a year?

Sales Manager: OK, I can live with that.

NOTE: Students require a wide range of expressions. For this reason, encourage experimentation and do not criticize inaccuracy during the activity. At the end, you can pick up points that were generally done badly.

## Payment

Explain that these activities are not just to help students understand how to use words connected with payment. They are also to help them use reference books — in this case a dictionary — to find information about how English works. In this way they can become more independent of the teacher.

## 1, 2 and 3

**ANSWERS**
(For more information refer the students to the relevant box of USING A DICTIONARY.)

1 For pay (noun) there is only one meaning. For pay (verb) there are three meanings.

2

| | |
|---|---|
| /peɪ/ | how we pronounce the word |
| noun (U) | an uncountable noun (i.e., you can't say *two pays*) |
| Hand symbol | a note giving related vocabulary |
| verb (pt, pp paid) | past tense and past participle are 'paid' |
| (I,T) | intransitive (doesn't take a direct object), transitive |
| pay (sb) (for sth) | pay somebody for something; you can but don't have to use the word in brackets |

3
1 Correct — uncountable, so singular.
2 Correct — past participle form after *be*.
3 Pay *by* — *by* with method of payment.
4 Correct — pay can take a direct object.
5 Paid *for* — *for* with object purchased.
6 Paid them $4,000 for the goods — money before item. *(We paid them $4,000 for the goods.)*
7 Correct — infinitive after *pay* in this meaning.

# SKILLS WORK

## Speaking 1

**1** As in Student's Book.

**PX** Alternative for pre-experience students: can you remember a time when you have had to negotiate — to reach a compromise? What did you want? What did the other person want? What was the compromise?

**2** Let students read the introduction. Then ask why it doesn't say: ~~Here are three advices~~. (*Advice* is uncountable so must be singular. To break it up we must use *pieces*.)

Students discuss and grade the pieces of advice. (There is no one right answer.)

## 3, 4 and 5

NOTE: In different organizational cultures negotiators are taught to perform a number of tasks. Check how well your students have covered these points (or if they have a different attitude to negotiation):

Prepare well for the negotiation.

Elicit/suggest possible solutions or ways of meeting needs.

Package the preferred option.

Propose implementing the solution or providing the product/service as per the package.

Deal with any outstanding difficulties.

Review the deal.

Get it in writing.

## Speaking 2

**1** If students can represent their own companies, they have the necessary background knowledge which any negotiator should bring to the negotiating table.

**2** Additional points might be:

Goods/Services: repairs and maintenance, spare parts, quality standards

Delivery: import duty

Payment: letters of credit.

**3** Additional points might be:

Customer: volume discount, particular international standards, firm delivery schedule

Supplier: advanced payment of part of the value, quick settlement of invoices, repeat orders, flexibility on delivery schedule.

**4** This is a fluency activity. Encourage students to take risks with the language they know — or half know. Success should be judged by how well the negotiation took place and by how well the two sides understood the agreement which was reached.

SUPPLEMENTARY ACTIVITY: Ask students to put their understanding of the agreement in writing. Compare the written versions and deal with confusion or misinterpretations. Point out that 'getting it in writing' is the vital final stage of any negotiation.

## Listening

**1 and 2**

Students in groups discuss the questions. Each group suggests a solution before listening to the second part of the account, after the beep.

As you go through the solutions on the tape, ask students if they think these were the best solutions or if their own were better. Ask why.

**ANSWERS**
Problem: getting the manager to put stock on display;

solution: boarding up the stockroom.

| | | |
|---|---|---|
| 2/1 | Problem: | removing safety guards while cleaning machines; |
| | Solution: | turning off the machines to frighten the operators. |
| 2/2 | Problem: | unions refusing to link payincrease to productivity deal; |
| | Solution: | sacking all the workers and offering them a new contract. |
| 2/3 | Problem: | not knowing how much to charge for a speech; |
| | Solution: | after finding out how many people were coming, charging three times normal fee. |

NOTE: In each case, the morality (or lack of it) of the managers' decisions should provoke an animated discussion! Make the most of this.

**3** If students are struggling, give them the definitions from the answers in jumbled order and remind them of the contexts.

**ANSWERS**

1  I was angry and didn't want the problem to continue.
2  It worked without any problems.
3  It gave them a big fright.
4  They refused to change their position.
5  They agreed — literally in this case by signing the new contracts.
6  I had no idea.

CLOSURE: Follow the procedure on page 11.

## PRESENTATION

> **Optional equipment and materials**
> sets of alphabet cards for exercise 4

**1** [cassette] Ask students to look at the illustration and ask quick questions about it:

| | |
|---|---|
| *What is it?* | an invoice |
| *Who is it to?* | Torres Mondano or Autorecambios Torrejón |
| *Who is it from?* | Crawley Electronics |
| *How much is it for?* | 3729.68 |

**PX** ALTERNATIVE PRESENTATION: Write the word *invoice* on the board and elicit/teach the purpose of an invoice — a request for payment of a certain amount for a list of things which have been ordered.

Ask students what they would expect to find on an invoice — make sure they get at least *who to; who from; date; quantity; goods; amount; payment terms.* (In some countries invoices must be signed; in many they must have tax registration details.)

Get students to find the things they have listed on the invoice in the Student's Book. Then check numbers and how to say the items as below. Remember to say numbers in the correct way for their purpose, i.e., *8-9-9-2-5* but *three thousand.*

| Teacher | Student |
|---|---|
| 4/7482 | That's the account number |
| 89925 | That's the invoice number |
| G/978 | That's the reference number of the Rapidex plugs |
| 0.54 | That's the unit cost of the Posilock pins |
| 3,000 | That's the number (quantity) of the Posilock connectors required |
| 3729.68 | That's the total due/to pay after discount |
| 30 | That's the number of days you have to pay |

As extra practice you could then choose some of the things and ask for the number, e.g., *What's the account number?*

Students read the instructions then play the tape once.

Let them compare answers in pairs before eliciting the whole class, but do not confirm or deny. Play the tape again, stopping at the relevant place to get the correct answer.

**ANSWERS**

| | |
|---|---|
| Rapidex plugs | ref J not G; size 7.92mm not 6.35 |
| Posilock connectors | 3500 not 3000 |
| Discount | 10% not 8% |
| Name | Montano not Mondano |

Ask students to remember the solutions to these problems. If necessary play the relevant parts again.

**ANSWERS**

| | |
|---|---|
| Rapidex plugs | Crawley are going to dispatch immediately; Autorecambios Torrejón are going to send back the others. |
| Posilock connectors | Crawley are going to send rest immediately. |
| Discount | Crawley are going to check. |

**2** [cassette] Students read the instructions and Extract 1. Play the tape until most students have identified most of the missing words.

Repeat for Extract 2.

**ANSWERS**

*Extract 1*
you dispatched the second one
whether it includes

*Extract 2*

| | |
|---|---|
| which was dispatched | The person I spoke to |
| how that happened | who deals with that |
| Was there anything else? | when she'll be back? |

Students check their answers carefully in pairs.

KEY LANGUAGE POINT: Point out the difference between direct and polite question forms:

*When did you dispatch ...*
*Could you tell me when you dispatched ...*

Point out that yes/no (closed) questions need an extra word — *if/whether* — to replace the deleted *do/does/did.*

Point out the sentence, beginning with the same structure as a statement, that also has a hidden question:

I don't know how that happened.

**3** Ask students to explain why the wrong size of Rapidex plugs was ordered (mispronunciation of G and J.) Elicit other differences with the way letter names are pronounced in the students' languages and English. Ask students to pronounce the whole alphabet in pairs. Ask students whose language has a non-Roman alphabet (eg., Japanese, Arabic) to explain how their writing system works.

**4** Make sure students pronounce the example words correctly and understand the task. If you have time, make sets of alphabet cards so that students can actually move cards into correct columns. Otherwise complete the chart on the board.

Students check with the file.

Drill the sounds in each column.

Highlight common difficulties
( B–P–V;   C–S–Z;   E–I;   A–H–R;   G–J).

# LANGUAGE WORK

> **Optional equipment and materials**
> Addresses for dictation in exercise 2, page 68
> Authentic business documents, word cards for exercise 1, page 69
> Word cards for exercise 1, page 70

## Pronunciation

If necessary, remind students of what they learnt in the final exercise in Presentation.

**1** 🔲 Play the conversation twice if necessary.

**ANSWER**
Avenida do Zimbabwe

**2** Students decide the answer in pairs. Play the tape again to check the answer and ask why that letter is stressed.

**ANSWER**
Because it is the 'new' (corrected) information.

If you have time, prepare other addresses for students to dictate, write down and, where appropriate, practise stressing misheard letters.

KEY LANGUAGE POINT: Stress in sentences is not only used to highlight the important 'information carrying' words. It is also used to highlight 'new' information for the listener.

**3** 🔲 **ANSWERS**

| | | | |
|---|---|---|---|
| 1 | C should be K | 4 | I should be Y |
| 2 | J should be H | 5 | B should be V |
| 3 | G should be J | | |

## Checking and Correcting

**1** **ANSWERS**

| Questions: | Replies: |
|---|---|
| OK? | Yes, fire away. |
| Was that...? | No, I said... |
| Was there anything else? | Yes, that's it. |
| Can I read that back to you? | |

When students have correctly filled in the spaces, ask them to cover the first column and try to remember *why* you use these questions, e.g.,

OK? — *Checking the other person is ready.*

With a less advanced class, go through all the expressions as a whole class activity. Then get students to write the answers themselves.

**2** Point out that the phrases in exercise 1 often occur in that order in a conversation. Give students time to prepare for their roles and assist where necessary.

## Documents

**1** Check comprehension, perhaps with a 'Many a Slip' game (see page 28). Focus on: procedures; documents; goods; transaction.

**PX** Explain to pre-experience students that you are going to look at different 'documents' used in business. Get students to identify examples — authentic if possible.

Prepare cards with the words on so students can move the words first into buyer and seller columns and then into chronological order. OR, students label the words B or S. Check with whole class before students put them in order.

**ANSWERS**

| Buyer: | Seller: |
|---|---|
| letter of enquiry | — |
| — | quotation |
| order | — |
| — | delivery note |
| — | invoice |
| — | reminder |
| cheque | — |
| — | receipt |

**PX** NOTE: A copy of the order is sometimes sent with the invoice. Invoices are sometimes sent before, sometimes with, the delivery. Reminders are only sent after the expiry of the period stated in the payment terms.

What is the purpose of each document? Students work in pairs to explain. Ask what might happen if any of the documents is not sent.

Possible answers

| 1 | Letter of enquiry | to find out if goods are available |
| 2 | Quotation | to give a price and conditions of sale |
| 3 | Order | to ask for goods. |
| 4 | Delivery note | to confirm what has been sent |
| 5 | Invoice | to ask for payment |
| 6 | Reminder | to ask again for payment |
| 7 | Cheque | to pay |
| 8 | Receipt | to acknowledge payment |

**2** See Student's Book.

## Explanations

**1** Point out that you often have to explain customs and words in your culture to foreign visitors. Work through one example. Students check in pairs before correcting their own answers with the file.

Write each of the words and explanations on a separate card/sheet. Give each student one word

and one explanation. Students have to try to find their two partners, without showing their words or explanations. This procedure is good for using spoken language.

**2** Highlight the grammar of the example:

*Ramadan is a month of the year when Muslims fast ...*

X is / a Y / when Z happens.

Focus on the use of *when* for time or period of time. Set the activity.

NOTE: Point out that *fast* is a verb in this context. Ask what *to fast* means, then replace the final part of the sentence with *... when Muslims don't eat or drink.*

**ANSWERS**

**1** who, that
**2** which, that
   (*That* can be used for people or things.)
**3** where
**4** whose

KEY LANGUAGE POINT: The structure of these relative clauses is quite complex. Make sure students recognize the key features:

Foreign word + *is/are* + generic type (e.g., *person*) + relative pronoun (e.g., *who*) + present simple explanation

**3** Put students from the same culture in groups to think up words and explanations. If students are from different cultures, help them write the explanation for one custom each, then use the 'Mix and Mingle' procedure (see exercise 1 above).

**4** Students work out their explanation before working in pairs. Encourage students to use relative clauses even where other structures are possible, e.g.,

not *Profit = Opposite of loss*

but *It's money you make when you sell something for more than you paid for it.*

## Enquiries

Remind students of the indirect questions from the conversation. Work through the examples asking students to identify key features, e.g.,

*No **does** in the first transformation*

*The word **is** at the end in the second transformation*

*If/whether in the third transformation*
(because it is a *yes/no* 'closed' question)

Check students' answers to 1 before they start pairwork. Students choose what phrase to use to begin the indirect question, depending on how likely it is that the listener will know the information (see exercise 2, Student's Book page 67, Grammar and Usage Notes, page 185).

**ANSWERS**

Could you tell me ...When the next train to Bristol is?

Do you know ...What time it gets there?

Have you any idea ...If there is a dining car on the train?

# SKILLS WORK

> **Optional equipment and materials**
> Handout of order form on page 72

## Speaking

Put the students into groups A and B. Group A looks at information on page 72. Group B looks at File 7 on page 153.

Help each group understand their instructions and authentic material. Remind students of telephone language they have learnt in this unit.

Group A should consider what questions they will need to ask to complete the order form — if possible, give a photocopy of the order form for the students to fill in.

Group B should practise saying the items they wish to order and asking for current prices.

Pair A students with B students. If feasible put them back-to-back so they have to communicate entirely through speaking.

Check the order forms/books and see if they make sense!

## Reading

1 Students read the introduction. Ask them to paraphrase to check they understand. Get the students to tell you why the mistakes are funny — don't kill the humour by focusing too much on what they should have said.

**ANSWERS**

It's funny because...

1 It sounds as if he was driving at the fly.
2 You can't collide with a tree you don't have.
3 It sounds as if he deliberately hit the pedestrian.
4 The use of *little, small, big* is funny. Also the idea that these things could cause an accident.
5 Normally we say 'I hit a pedestrian'.
6 It sounds as if he was driving continuously for 40 years.
7 You normally swerve to miss, not hit, someone.
8 Something which is stationary can't be coming the other way.
9 Signs can't suddenly appear.
10 The result does not follow from the reason.
11 We normally use 'found by' some people not 'animals'.
12 Invisible cars don't exist.

As a recap activity, ask students to close their books and try to remember 20 words from this section connected with roads and accidents.

2 General discussion. See Student's Book.

CLOSURE: Follow the procedure on page 11.

41

# PRESENTATION

**1** Give students time to discuss the questions; if all the students are from the same department of the same company, this is a good opportunity to find out information which will be useful for later activities. If they are from different companies or from different parts of the same company, get them to try to find things in common, e.g., *Most visitors who speak English are from Germany; most of the business trips are to attend conferences in English.*

**PX** You will have to omit this activity with pre-experience classes. Exploit the visuals to set the scene for the conversation.

**2** ▭ This is a fun activity — you do not normally have to work out what people are talking about without even being able to see them — but it focuses attention on key words, an important listening skill.

Play each conversation straight through and then let students work in pairs to compare their ideas; do a whole class feedback but do not confirm or deny any of the ideas; play the tape again and stop at the important points to check the answers.

### ANSWERS

1   Mrs Sandbulte, receptionist, in an office building at the reception area, a business card
2   Louise (the hostess) and her husband, Ulla and Kjell (the guests), in a house, a bunch of flowers
    NOTE: the flowers are chrysanthemums, associated in Mediterranean countries with death, but in the UK it is fine to give them.
3   A rail passenger and his/her host, at a railway station, a book
4   Two business people, one called Sam; at a golf course; a golf club
5   A hotel receptionist and guest (Mrs Haberland); in a hotel at the reception; a fax

**3** ### ANSWERS

Could I
Sure
Would you like to
May I
I'm afraid.

**4** If possible, get some of the better pairs to act out the conversation in front of the class; do not criticize for grammar but point out any problems with the social encounter, e.g., embarrassing pauses.

**5** ### ANSWERS

*From the conversation:*
You're welcome.
Not at all.

*Other:*
Don't mention it.
That's OK.
It was nothing.
It was a pleasure.

*From the conversation:*
Now I insist on paying for this.

*Other answer:*
Please let me give you something for this.

SUPPLEMENTARY ACTIVITY: Ask students how they would reply if someone said *Sorry*.

Possible answers:

*Don't worry about it.*
*It doesn't matter.*
*It's not important.*
*No harm done.*

**6** ### ANSWERS

Good shot! Well done!
Hard luck.
1 hitting   2 getting   3 visiting   4 seeing.

**7** ### ANSWERS

extending   Would   leaving   Shall.

Ask students the reason for the *-ing* endings on many words in the last two exercises. (Verb endings are often affected by words that come before. Here: preposition; gerund.)

**8** Work through the first two as examples. Encourage students to use *interesting* verbs to complete the sentences.

# LANGUAGE WORK

## Polite Phrases

**1** Ask students to list all the modal verbs they know; if they are stuck give them one example then proceed as in Student's Book.

**ANSWERS**
1  could, would, can, will
2  could, may, can

Ask students to work out any rules for using these words in requests. The possible rules are:

*Would* can only be used with *you* requests.
*May* can only be used with *I*.
*Could* and *can* can be used with either.

Ask students why we have different ways of saying the same thing.

**ANSWER**
We need more polite forms for people we don't know well, for larger or more difficult requests, and for important occasions.

**2** Let students read the introduction then check understanding of the word *formal*, e.g., *Why are we formal? How do we show this?*

Act out conversation 1 with a good student, exaggerating the rudeness. Elicit from the whole class ways of making it more polite.

Allow plenty of time and let students argue about what level of politeness is necessary/appropriate in each case.

NOTE: Point out that in English a request is rarely refused outright, e.g., *I'd like to help, but...*

**POSSIBLE ANSWERS**
1  **V**  Could I speak to Erling Lund?
   **R**  May I have your name?
   **V**  Yes, it's Kate Williams. I'm afraid I'm in rather a hurry.
   **R**  I'm sorry but he's in a meeting at the moment. Would you mind waiting a moment? There's a seat over there.
2  **R**  Could you sign the visitors' book please?
   **V**  Of course. May I use your pen?

   **R**  Certainly. Would you like some coffee?
   **V**  I'm afraid I don't drink coffee. Do you have any tea?
3  **V**  Could you possibly put my briefcase somewhere safe?
   **S**  Certainly.
   **V**  I wonder if I might have another cup of tea?
   **S**  Of course. Please help yourself.
4  **V**  Could I see your customer address list?
   **C**  I'd like to help but I'm afraid it's confidential.
   **V**  Really? I thought your colleague Mr Lopez said I could.
   **C**  I'm afraid there must have been a mistake.

## Pronunciation

**1**   Put students in pairs and ask one student to read the introduction and explain it to the other student; check and correct if necessary, then play the tape. Ask students to explain any differences they hear.

Point out the flat intonation and small pitch range of the second sentence. Get students to imitate both sentences.

NOTE: In some languages (e.g., Swiss German) a wide pitch range in the male voice denotes effeminacy. However, in polite British or American English small pitch range will be interpreted as rudeness, however polite the actual words spoken.

**2**   **ANSWERS**
1  **a**  rude    **b**  polite
2  **a**  polite    **b**  rude
3  **a**  rude    **b**  polite
4  **a**  rude    **b**  polite
5  **a**  rude    **b**  polite
6  **a**  polite    **b**  rude

Again, get students to imitate the two versions. Ask them to provide adjectives to describe the two speakers, e.g., 1a aggressive, 2b impatient.

## Showing Interest

1 Questions need not necessarily fit into the list of categories given.

2 Practise the positive noises with polite intonation — often rising to show interest — before students converse in pairs. If necessary use negative checking — showing *dis*interest through bored intonation.

Elicit/teach also some polite negatives for the 'host', e.g.,

*I'm afraid I don't know.*
*I'm sorry — I'm not very good at (history).*
*I'm not really sure ( but I'll find out for you ).*

If possible, get pairs to have conversations in front of the class.

3 Get students to name the tenses used before reading the question under the conversation.

Elicit/remind how to construct the present perfect from the auxiliary *have* and the past participle; that regular past participles have the same form as the past tense. With a less advanced group, drill the formation of the past participle of irregular verbs, e.g., *meet — met, see — seen*, etc. Give them time to try to write the grammar rules.

4 Ask students why we often begin conversations with *Have you ...*

Drill the questions up to the past participle, focusing on the weak form of *Have* and the rising intonation to the topic.

Point out that in the conversation practice an answer *Yes* opens the way to definite questions, e.g., *When, How, Why, What ...*, about the topic.

KEY LANGUAGE POINT: If students raise the use of *before, yet* and *ever* with the present perfect, be prepared to explain:

*Before* is really looking backward from an event in the present, e.g.,

You are visiting the company now. *Have you visited it before?*

*Yet* is used when the speaker doesn't know if the event has happened or not, e.g.,

*Have you met the Managing Director yet?*

Commonly, *yet* is used where the event is planned or expected and will happen in the future if it hasn't happened already.

*Ever* is used when the speaker doesn't know if the event has happened or not, or if it is planned or expected, e.g.,

*Have you ever eaten octopus?*

## Socializing

1 Give students as long as they wish to think of possible replies; when you feel they are getting stuck, go on to 2.

NOTE: Number 10 could be saying that something interesting happened rather than a criticism. With a strong class demonstrate how intonation would change the meaning.

2 It is useful to have a range of fixed expressions to cover good and bad news, praise and criticism, etc. These expressions do not need to be analysed for grammatical form — it is more important that students learn to recognize the type of information they are being given so they can respond correctly and fluently with the appropriate phrase.

**ANSWERS**
1 e    2 f    3 h    4 j    5 b    6 d    7 a    8 c    9 g    10 i

For students who have to do a lot of socializing in their work, put these replies on the board and ask the students what statements might prompt them:

I'll drink to that!
That's fantastic. We must celebrate.
Nothing serious, I hope?
Oh, on what subject?
Have you taken any aspirins?
Let me help you look.
Don't worry, I will.
I know, I'm terribly sorry. Something came up.
Oh dear. What a shame!
Lucky you!

## Cultural Differences

Set the preamble and instructions in 1 as a reading activity with the following questions to answer:

1 The text mentions two things which can cause problems. What are they? (*Language mistakes; misunderstandings between cultures.*)

2 What is the purpose of this task? (*To consider how behaviour varies between cultures.*)

3 In the task, where are you? (*At an international conference.*)

4 What can you talk about? (*Anything you like.*)

5 What should you do now? (*Talk to the other participants, following the relevant set of rules.*)

1 Help people to prepare for the role play; the better the preparation, the better the role play. The actual role play will probably last only a few minutes. It is better if students do not read ahead to exercise 2.

2 (If students are stuck, ask them to think about the areas in 3 below.) There is no right answer to the first question as the files do not describe particular cultures.

How we respond to cultural differences is perhaps the most important question. Try to elicit some examples of how cultural signals can be misinterpreted, e.g.,

*Talking loudly = angry;*
*not making eye contact = lying.*

Make the point that speaking a new language means learning a new culture as well.

3 Encourage anecdotes from well-travelled students.

You could also discuss differences in attitudes to time and appointments, and hand signs.

ALTERNATIVE ACTIVITIES:

1 With a multi-cultural class ask students to explain in mixed culture groups what they think the rules of their culture are, e.g.,

*In my culture we stand close to each other.*

2 With a mono-cultural class, ask students to decide in small groups what the rules of their culture are, then compare groups' ideas.

# SKILLS WORK

**Equipment and materials**
Counters/tokens for game on page 81

## Speaking

The Travel Game is designed to encourage students to use some of the language they have learnt so far (should also be fun!). They will probably get as much language practice out of arguing over the rules and discussing what they have to do — provided they do it in English — as they will from the language forfeits.

ALTERNATIVE PROCEDURE: Play the game in threes — the third person adjudicates and decides if the language is OK. If not, you miss a go.

## Listening

1 As an alternative to the procedure in the Student's Book — set up groups, have a time limit for each question and give points equal to the number of correct items in each category.

**POSSIBLE ANSWERS**
(your students may think of more)
1 beef, lamb, mutton, pork, bacon
2 turkey, chicken, duck
3 salmon, trout, plaice, cod
4 crab, lobster, prawn, oyster
5 thyme, basil, tarragon, marjoram
6 frying, boiling, grilling, roasting

2 Ask students to put their hands up when they have found the answers, but not to call out. When most people have raised their hand, ask the first to do so.

**ANSWERS**
1 Melon, blackcurrant
2 Spinach, avocado, lettuce, tomatoes, mushrooms, beanshoots
3 Breast of chicken
4 Fillet of turbot
5 Prawns
6 Parsley
7 Ginger
8 Charcoal grilled, stir-fried

45

**3** [cassette] Check answers, then ask what students are going to have, and what it is.

**ANSWERS**

The man is going to have savoury pancakes followed by lamb cutlets.

The woman is going to have soup of the day or melon followed by breast of chicken.

NOTE: In English we say *I'll have...* or *I'm going to have...* when we are ordering food, not *eat* or *take*.

SUPPLEMENTARY ACTIVITY: Put the students in threes to act out the conversation with the waiter or waitress when they come to take the order.

**4** Point out that *type*, *kind*, and *sort* are near-synonyms.

**5** The only possible problem here is spelling. See if they can think of some more words to describe food ending in *–y*.

**ANSWERS**

Salty; fatty (double *t* because word ends consonant-vowel-consonant); vinegary; smoky.

Other examples: spicy; tangy; sugary (not sweety!); syrupy; peppery; fiery.

**6** If students struggle with this activity, check/teach the meanings of the prepositions with a matching activity. Indicate something in the classroom (e.g., a table) and ask students for the correct preposition:

It's made   *of* wood (what the ingredient(s) are)
*from* trees (what the ingredient(s) were originally)
*in* Spain (where it was made)
*by* machine (how to make it)
*up of* a top and four legs (what the components are — separate parts)

**7** With a monocultural class, ask different groups to describe different dishes, perhaps making up a complete menu.

With multicultural classes, put students in groups to tell each other.

Question the groups at the end to see which food they would like to eat from the descriptions they heard.

CLOSURE: Follow the procedure on page 11.

## PRESENTATION

> **Optional equipment and materials**
> OHT of basic project chart for exercise 1, page 84

Ask students to say what is happening in each illustration, and what the connection is between the activities.

They are all part of a large project.

**1** Ask students to discuss answers in pairs/groups then report to whole class. Don't confirm or correct.

If the ideas aren't very good, check comprehension of the chart conventions by asking a few questions:

1 How many weeks are shown? (*fifteen*)
2 How many activities? (*six*)
3 When should installation begin? (*Week 9*)
4 How long should it take? (*2 weeks*)
5 What should begin in the sixth week (two activities)? (*Site preparation and recruiting operators*)
6 How is it possible to begin two activities in the same week? (*Because (a) they involve different people and (b) you don't have to finish one before you can start the other*)
7 Why does site preparation begin in week 6 not week 1? (*Because you have got to finish the feasibility study before you can begin the site preparation*)

Ask students the advantages of planning a project like this.

(You can make sure everyone knows what should happen and when. You can follow progress and see if things are happening on time. If they are happening late or early, you know what activities must be put back or brought forward. It is easy to read.)

**2** 🔲 Ask students to read the instructions and check they understand the task. Play the tape and give time to write answers. Check the answers. Ask how they got the answers and if necessary play the tape again, stopping at the critical points which are:

1 *When did you place the order? — At the end of week five.*
2 *Did they deliver on schedule? — Yes, everything arrived at the end of week eight. But they won't finish installing it until the end of week eleven —But that's another two weeks.*
3 *So this date for the change-over ...*

**ANSWERS**
1 Triangle = place order, circle = deliver equipment, star = change-over (from old equipment to new)
2 It is week 9
3 Put off change-over for one week, to the end of week 12

Mark week 9 on the chart and ask some questions to check understanding and grammar.

It's week 9 now so:

1 What have they done so far?
2 What haven't they done yet?
3 What are they doing at the moment?
4 What are they going to do next and when?

**3** 🔲 Give students time to read the questions and to think about possible answers before playing tape.

**ANSWERS**
1 To deliver and install the equipment within 5 weeks.
2 They delivered the equipment.
3 There is a dispute about this.
4 They're being given theoretical training.
5 It can't risk changing over without tests.

**4** Put the two examples on the board without the italicized words and see if students can complete them. The second verb in a clause will not be in a tense. Explain there are no rules about this — they must learn which form (infinitive or gerund) for the second verb when they learn a verb.

**ANSWERS**

| | | | |
|---|---|---|---|
| 1 | to deliver | 5 | installing |
| 2 | to prepare | 6 | giving |
| 3 | having | 7 | changing |
| 4 | to get | 8 | to put |

Write the first verbs in two rows on board:

| | |
|---|---|
| guarantee<br>choose<br>manage<br>want | to do |
| deny<br>finish<br>carry on<br>risk | doing |

Suggest students record vocabulary in this way:

*guarantee + to do*; *deny + -ing*

# LANGUAGE WORK

> **Optional equipment and materials**
>
> Products, advertisements, etc., from Body Shop for exercise 1, page 88
>
> Advertisements, brochures, etc. from Procter and Gamble for exercise 1, page 92

## Developments

Ask students to read the introduction and to explain:

*Who is doing what in the first part (up to the comma)?*
(Governments ... introducing ... legislation)

*Who is doing what in the second part?*
(Auto manufacturers ... researching ... electric vehicles)

*What is the relationship between the two activities?*
(Electric vehicles are more environmentally friendly;

they use up fewer hydrocarbons and don't pollute the atmosphere.)

Double check vocabulary:

*What is legislation?* (laws)

*What is environmental legislation?*
(laws about protecting the world we live in)

*What is stricter environmental legislation?*
(stronger laws ...)

1 Ask students to look at the illustration and the headline and say what they think the article will be about. Ask them to read the introduction to the exercise and carry out the task. Perhaps add extra pre-reading questions:

*Why did the electric car become unpopular?*
*Why is it a good time to drive an electric car now?*

**ANSWERS**
Since the turn of the century, i.e., about 1900.
There were new inventions for the gasoline-powered car.
Because electricity is safe and clean.

2 Ask students to read the instructions then do the first one with them as an example.

NOTE: Questions 2 to 5 practise past tense question forms in preparation for language work later. Deal with any problems over construction.

**ANSWERS**
1 Is the electric car a new invention?
2 When did Detroit Edison have fleets of electric vehicles?
3 How many electric cab fleets did they operate?
4 What was everyone talking about at the Electric Light Convention in 1911?
5 What did Henry Ford do in 1912?

3 Give students time. Prompt if necessary, so that they are ready to read the advertisement in 4 critically.

**POSSIBLE ANSWERS**
Not very powerful, can't go very far without recharging, nowhere to recharge, batteries are heavy, takes a long time to recharge

**4** This is quite a complex text considering it is an advertisement! Make sure students extract the key information:

1 Cars with this battery can go 100 miles without recharging.
2 A 50% recharge takes eight minutes.
3 These batteries cost less than other types.

If necessary give this information and ask students to find exactly where the advertisement gives it.

**5** Use procedures as for 2 above.

**ANSWERS**
1 What's this advertisement for?
2 What has stopped public acceptance of the electric vehicle?
3 What has Electrosource done?
4 What have many independent tests confirmed?
5 Has any company solved the second part of the problem?

**6 ANSWERS**

*Simple past*
said (colloquial expression!), supported, had, was put (simple past but passive), started, conquered.

*Present perfect*
has stalled, has solved(2), have confirmed.

**7** KEY LANGUAGE POINTS:

1 We know when each of the simple past things happened — check this by asking, e.g., *When did Detroit Edison support fleets of electric vehicles?*

2 We don't know when each of the present perfect things happened or started — check this by asking, e.g., *When did Electrosource solve the problem?*

Students could identify each use of the present perfect on page 173.

SUPPLEMENTARY ACTIVITIES: Find a noun for each verb.

charge (*a battery*)
solve (*a problem*)
fund (*a development*)
confirm (*a result*)
operate (*a fleet*)

## A social action programme

**1** General discussion — it doesn't matter if students haven't heard of The Body Shop, but some products, brochures, etc., would be nice!

**PX** Ask pre-experience students:

*How can a company create a good impression in the market?*

Elicit at least the following, by prompting if necessary: making good products, telling people about the products, having good staff relations, having good customer care, supporting local events — sponsorship.

Then do exercise 1 above.

**2** Ask students what they think a *social action programme* is. Don't confirm or correct at this stage.

Suggest students read the whole thing through before trying to fill in the verbs, but remind them of the two ways of talking about the past. Direct their attention to the time or time reference which is given, e.g., *in 1976* — simple past, *since the beginning* — present perfect.

**ANSWERS**
opened, have now grown, have been, won, signed, brought, funded, sold, has now progressed, started, has renovated and refurbished, has begun, have taken care, have been working, expanded.

**3** Give plenty of time for the discussion. The priority is to get the students talking.

**ANSWERS**
1 Activities to benefit local communities, campaigns, launch of a newspaper to help the homeless, a relief drive to help Romanian orphans.
2 No right answer but elicit/teach 'corporate image'.
3 Yes, there can be, because of the good corporate image — people who buy Body Shop products are the same socio-economic class who are concerned about these issues.

**4/5** Encourage students to say something.

## Reporting back

Remind students of the two forms for the second verb in a clause, including the names infinitive and gerund. Then follow Student's Book.

**ANSWERS**

| | | | |
|---|---|---|---|
| 1 to achieve | 5 losing | 9 to run |
| 2 to reach | 6 reducing | 10 to cut |
| 3 being | 7 lowering | 11 making |
| 4 to get | 8 to reduce | 12 to wait |

Write the verbs in two rows, this time asking students to do it from memory.

| offer | | suggest | |
|---|---|---|---|
| manage | | delay | |
| fail | to do | help | doing |
| refuse | | avoid | |
| hope | | keep on | |
| afford | | | |
| agree | | | |

NOTE: *help* meaning *aid/assist* is followed by *to do*.

## Financial Results

*Information on balance sheets and profit and loss accounts*

A balance sheet shows the state of a company's finances at a particular moment in time. It balances what the company owns—its assets, against what it owes—its liabilities. A profit and loss account shows the income and expenditure of a company over a period of time, usually a year.

In the example, Index Engineering's assets (the things it owns) appear in the left-hand column. These include the Fixed Assets (permanent, established assets) it needs to carry out its business, such as land, buildings, plant, and equipment. It also includes their investments in other companies. Then there are Current Assets—assets which can be converted quickly into cash. They include the goods made but not yet sold (Finished Goods), the products being made now (Work in Progress), money that other firms it trades with owe it (Debtors) and the money it has in the bank.

Index Engineering's liabilities appear at the top and bottom of the right-hand column. This is the money it owes other people or institutions. It is the money that has been put into the business to make it work.

Index Engineering has two types of liabilities.

1 *Current liabilities*: These are short term debts, money that must be paid back within a year. They include money borrowed from the bank (Bank Overdrafts and Loans), money it owes its suppliers (Trade creditors), money it has spent but hasn't handed over yet (Accrued expenses), other money owed to institutions such as the tax office (Other Creditors including taxation), and money it owes its shareholders (Dividend payable).

2 *Capital and Reserves*: This is the money shareholders have supplied (Share capital) and profit made and put back into the business (Profit and Loss Account).

Obviously, what a company owns should balance with what it owes. This calculation is done in the centre of the right-hand column in the example. First the Current Liabilities are subtracted from the Current Assets to give the Net Current Assets (Liabilities). Last year this was a positive sum. This year it is negative so it is written in brackets. Then the fixed assets are added to the total. The result balances with the money in Capital and Reserves.

Index Engineering's Profit and Loss Account shows the money it has received and paid out in the last year. It has three main parts:

1 *Income*: From sales (Turnover) and from money invested in other ventures (Investment income).

2 *Costs*: These are the costs it incurred in order to earn its income. They include Cost of Sales (the cost of buying raw materials and producing the goods it has sold), Administrative costs and other Overheads (for example, rent, light, heating, salaries), Interest payable (the money it paid banks etc., for loans) and also Depreciation (because Index Engineering's fixed assets have lost value over the year).

3 *Profit*: When the costs are subtracted from the income, the money left over is the profit, or if it is a negative figure (in brackets in the example) it is a loss. There are three types of profit/loss in the example, depending on whether tax and dividend payments have been subtracted.

The terms used in financial statements vary from company to company. For example, profits might be called *earnings* and share capital might be called *equity*. Also, the layout of documents varies, particularly between 'Latin' and 'Anglo Saxon'

50

countries. Students may find it interesting to compare their accounting documents with these standard UK examples.

Prepare for the activity as follows.

1 Check students understand the verbs to borrow and to lend. (If necessary, explain that borrowing is like temporary taking and lending is like temporary giving.) Then check they understand the verbs to own and to owe. (Ask who owns various items in the class. Borrow some money from a students and explain you owe them the money because you have to pay it back.)

2 Tell students they are going to look at a company's balance sheet and profit and loss account. Ask them to predict items the financial statements will contain. Give a few examples to start them off if necessary, for example, assets (what types?), liabilities, turnover. Do not explain or correct at this stage.

**PX** ALTERNATIVE FOR PRE-EXPERIENCE STUDENTS: Using the information above, explain the two documents, while students examine the examples in their book. Then ask them to check the figures (calculators are useful) making sure that the balance sheet 'balances' and working out which figures are added and subtracted to achieve the totals on the profit and loss account.

I Set the questions. With less experienced or pre-experienced students write the answers on the board and let them match them to the correct explanations.

**ANSWERS**
I   Assets and liabilities
2   Fixed Assets
3   Interest payable
4   Bank Overdrafts and loans
5   Share capital
6   Dividend payable
7   Trade creditors
8   Debtors
9   Turnover
10  Cost of sales
11  Accrued expenses
12  Administration and other overheads
13  Depreciation
14  Stocks

NOTE: On some balance sheets, shares are called *stocks*, but not here.

2 Also remind students of suitable verbs and then accept any correct sentences.

3 Refer students to the Profit and Loss Account to find evidence for the example.

**ANSWERS**
• Plant and Equipment up; Bank Overdrafts and Loans up
• Stocks of Finished Goods up
• Debtors up
• Trade creditors down
• Investment income down
• Dividends down

4 See Student's Book.

## Achievements

I General discussion — it doesn't matter if students haven't heard of Procter & Gamble, but brochures etc., would be nice!

2 Ask them what *environmental quality management* might mean.

Set global question.

**ANSWER**
Because you never stop improving.

SUPPLEMENTARY ACTIVITY: Quick comprehension questions.

1 Find three areas in which Procter & Gamble are trying to improve. (*Products, packaging, and operations*)

2 How have Procter & Gamble policies affected the environment? Find three verbs. (*protect — look after; preserve — keep it safe; enhance — make it better*)

3 Find four ways of achieving this. (*plan to reduce pollution; reduce waste; check results; establish systems*)

4 Find five divisions of Procter & Gamble. (*Corporate Buildings; Foods; Health and Beauty Care; Paper; Soap*)

5 Find which division is doing best in environmental management terms, which is worst and which improved most in 1991. (*best — corporate buildings; worst — health and beauty care; most improved — foods*)

51

Ask students to suggest reasons for the results shown in the chart.

Possible answers: Perhaps it is relatively easy to make buildings environmentally friendly, whereas a lot of health and beauty products involve chemicals and/or testing to animals, perhaps these and foods have been improved rapidly because of the consumer interest in this area.

Follow-up questions:

1  Why is it a quality improvement cycle? (*Because it is circular, from planning back to planning again.*)

2  What do you think the numbers on the graph refer to? (*Success ratings out of 10 in a company annual survey.*)

3  How do you think they are arrived at? (*Perhaps by comparing performance to a national standard in a number of areas — like recycling of waste products.*)

**3**  Give students plenty of time to come up with some ideas, then refer them to the Grammar Note.

**ANSWERS**
1  *Have been pursuing* — because we are still carrying out the action.

2  *Have achieved* — because we are interested in the completion of the action.

**4**  Focus on the two forms of the present perfect (simple and continuous) and their meanings/usage. Refer students to the relevant note in the Grammar and Usage Notes (page 173). Work through several examples and get the key part of the verb — the present participle or past participle — on the board.

*They've been recycling/making/sorting/using ...*
*They've saved/reduced/cut ...*

Give students time to complete some more cases. During feedback, get the remainder of the verb participles on the board.

**5**  Procedure as in Student's Book.

# SKILLS WORK

## Listening

**1**  Ask students to read the instructions. Stress that the students only have to identify the subjects during the first listening, not specific ideas.

With a less advanced class, write the subjects on the board in the wrong order and let students simply number them.

**2  ANSWERS**
unemployment
redundancies at Guinness
cigarette advertising
state retirement age
high speed trains

**3**  Ask students to read instructions. This is a key listening skill — the ability to identify when subjects change.

Deal with their answers and reactions to them.

In a one-to-one class let the student operate the tape recorder for this activity.

**ANSWERS**
1  3 million unemployed people, 40,000 increase this month.

2  Because the company is profitable.

3  A tobacco industry report says advertising only encourages people to switch brands; the Department of Health report says banning advertising would reduce consumption.

4  67; to cut the Social Security budget and allow more to be given to the over-80s.

5  Tie them to posts to see if maintenance teams can work while trains are running; BR staff and others who think it sounds exciting.

SUPPLEMENTARY ACTIVITY: Explain to students that *has done* is used for changes or news.

So what has happened since the last news broadcast?

What/who

1 has risen? (*unemployment*)

2 has been announced? (*700 redundancies*)

3 has hit back at what? (*the tobacco industry, at the Department of Health report*)

4 has called for what? (*an MP, for a higher retirement age*)

5 has been recruiting people for what? (*British Rail, for volunteers to test the effects of turbulence*)

## Pronunciation 🔲

Let students try to do the task by themselves, then check in pairs. Finally in whole class ask students to make the odd one out sound different.

Ask students if they can find any rules — there aren't many but it is useful for them to find this out for themselves.

**ANSWERS**

1  book = /ʊ/ not /uː/

2  suit = /uː/ not /ʌ/

3  met = /e/ not /ʌ/

4  shoot = /uː/ not /ʊ/

5  look = /ʊ/ not /ʌ/

6  come = /ʌ/ not /e/

*Possible 'rules'*

1  'u' before 'ck' = /ʌ/

2  'u' in other cases normally /uː/ (but see 'put')

3  'oo' can be /uː/ or /ʊ/

## Speaking

Spend as long as necessary on setting up this activity. Apart from anything else, it is an opportunity to revise vocabulary for the list of possible areas. If necessary, revise area meanings.

When students have chosen an area, deal with the method of presenting the information. Turn the items under *Describe* into sentences, e.g., *We aimed to improve.*

Give students time to prepare — perhaps until the next lesson.

CLOSURE: Follow the procedure on page 11.

## PRESENTATION

**1** Write SEASONS on the board and ask what the four seasons are; write the answers on the board.

VOCABULARY NOTE: *fall* is American English for *autumn*. Ask students to explain *seasonal*. Remind them to use words for the seasons not months.

VOCABULARY NOTE: *Toiletries* are cosmetics, soaps etc., (popular Christmas presents) and have no direct relationship with the modern meaning of the word *toilet*.

CULTURE NOTE: When a particular season occurs depends on where a country is, not on the month. Items like fireworks (used on November 5th in Britain) are seasonal because of festivals rather than the weather. So cultural behaviour plus climate creates seasonal fluctuations in markets.

**2** Students read the introduction. Ask questions, e.g.,

*What is the trend in diagram 1?* (downwards)
*What about graph 4?* (upwards)
*So, what is a trend?* (a movement up or down over time)

Point out that graphs show trends — it is difficult to 'see' a trend from a table of figures, like 2.

**PX** In pre-experience classes, set these questions for group discussion.

1 Why is it important for a business to find out about trends in the market? (*To help plan future operations.*)

2 What trends is it important for a business to find out about? (*Age profile of the population in their market; movement of people into or out of their area, and changes in social class. Changes in attitude towards products, e.g., fur products; their share of the market.*)

Do not confirm or correct answers. Explain that exercises 3 and 4 will help to check their ideas.

**3** ▭ Remind students that the graphs and tables are illustrations from the manager's talk — perhaps to his board of management. Pause after each extract to give students time to identify the matching illustration. With a weaker group, play each extract again. With a strong group, ask what key words helped them match illustration and extract.

**ANSWERS**

| Extract | Graph |
| --- | --- |
| 1 | 4 |
| 2 | 5 |
| 3 | 1 |
| 4 | 2 |
| 5 | 3 |

Check students' understanding of key words: *projection, sector, distribution, outlet, media, spend, shift, protection, budget.*

**4** **ANSWERS**

1 Advertising budget/media spend
2 Age shifts within the population
3 Sales by sector
4 Total Sales
5 Sales by distribution

**5** ▭

**PX** NOTE: Graphs tell you what happened or might happen, not why. You need other data to explain the trends.

VOCABULARY NOTE: Don't try to explain *cause and effect chain* until students have had a chance to work out the answers.

**ANSWER**

| A | B | C |
| --- | --- | --- |
| global warming | record levels of sunshine | growth in sales |

A *was the cause of* B — B *was the cause of* C
or
B *was the effect of* A — C *was the effect of* B

1 Growth in sales is largely due to record levels of sunshine.
2 Record levels of sunshine may be a result of global warming.

KEY LANGUAGE POINT: These expressions refer backwards, from effect to cause.

Forward reference, from cause to effect, can be achieved through different phrases using *cause* and *effect* (as above) or *result*:

*A may have caused/resulted in/had the effect of B; B resulted in C.*

**6** ▭ Use a 'deep-end' strategy — i.e., don't give any help or correction at this stage; just let them try to describe changes before listening.

**ANSWERS**
1   Some sales are rising rapidly, some have fallen slightly, some have remained steady.
2   People buy health-care products from chemists and sun care is becoming more popular with the rising numbers of deaths from cancer.

NOTE: The manager describes sector changes within distribution outlets. The graphs only show the global change.

**7** ▭ Refer students to graph 1. Do they notice anything strange? (In 1991, TV advertising only.) Then play the tape.

**ANSWERS**
1   TV shots (TV advertising)
2   No.
3   It can target consumers with a high income.

**8** ▭ Table 2 will help the gap fill. Do not check answers. Let students listen to talk 4 to check.

**ANSWERS**
Demographic; probably; likely; negative
21–30 group declining, 50+ group expanding

Check vocabulary by eliciting/teaching opposites:

*adverse/beneficial*
*negative/positive*

**9** ▭

Refer students to the pie chart (graph 3).

Make sure students understand: the complete 'pie' = 100%; the size of a piece of pie reflects the percentage share of market.

Play the tape.

**ANSWERS**
Sun protection creams and lotions account for the largest part; after-sun preparations are becoming slightly more important; the green and cruelty-free brand is selling well and will definitely grow.

Check vocabulary: turnover is the 'whole pie' in this case; *niche* = small, but well-defined and important.

Ask: *Why is green and cruelty free a 'niche' market?*

# LANGUAGE WORK

> **Optional equipment and materials**
> Graph for supplementary dictation activity suggested for exercise 4, page 102

## Discussing probability

**1** Remind students/get them to remember some predictions and projections from the last lesson.

**POSSIBLE ANSWERS**
4
3, e, c
1,6,
2, b, d
5, a, f

NOTE: This activity is easier to check, and probably more effective, if the sentences are cut up for students to rearrange.

KEY LANGUAGE POINTS:

1   When we have negative opinions we move negation from the idea to the introductory verb. Sometimes the negation is conveyed by using a 'negative' verb — e.g., *doubt*

| So | *I* | *think* | *it won't happen* |
|---|---|---|---|
| becomes | *I* | *don't think* | *it will happen* |
| or | *I* | *doubt if* | *it will happen* |

2   *Could* and *might* have similar meaning in the positive in this case:

   *It might happen*
   *It could happen*

   but note how the meaning changes in the negative:

   *It might not happen* = there is a chance it won't
   *It could not happen* = impossible

3   *May* is theoretically more likely than *might*. In practice some English speakers rarely use *may*; it is very uncommon in the negative *may not*.

**2**   Check some of the conversations in pairs at the end.

KEY LANGUAGE POINTS:

1   The statement becomes a request for a prediction:

| | *We* | *have another Gulf War* |
|---|---|---|
| *Do you think* | *we could* | *have another Gulf War?* |

2   *I'm afraid* introduces an unhappy future possibility. If, in your view, the possible future event is positive, it can be replaced by *I think/ I'm sure/I expect*.

3   Notice the use of *there* in sentence 9.

## Market Movements

**I**   ANSWERS

| STEM | MOVEMENT | PAST | PAST PARTICPLE |
|---|---|---|---|
| decrease | down | decreased | decreased |
| fall | down | fell | fallen |
| rise | up | rose | risen |
| raise | up | raised | raised |

**2**   ANSWERS

| | | | |
|---|---|---|---|
| I | Raised | 4 | Raised |
| 2 | Rises | 5 | Rose |
| 3 | Risen | 6 | Raise |

Emphasize the 'someone did it / it happened' difference by asking after each answer – *Who did it?*

**3**   Let students discuss the 'good or bad news' question. Clearly, it is a question of your point of view whether any movement is good or bad. *Pepsi sales jump* is bad news for Coca-cola! With a strong class get students to tell you the two sides in each case, e.g.,

*Land prices soar* is good news for farmers, and bad news for the construction industry probably.

NOTE: Most verbs for movement do not indicate the writer or speaker's point of view. Exceptions are:

| good movements: | *improve, gain, strengthen, steady* |
|---|---|
| bad movements: | *worsen, decline, plunge, plummet, slump, weaken, rocket* |

**4**   BUSINESS NOTES:

1   Countries either have a trade deficit (buy more than they sell) or surplus (sell more than they buy) with other countries.

2   'Big Blue' is IBM — because it is big and has a blue logo.

3   After recession there is a recovery.

Other verb opposites are:

   jump/slump
   take off/dip
   soar/plunge
   rocket/tumble
   improve/worsen
   gain/lose
   weaken/strengthen
   shrink/expand

Only some verbs can be used as or made into nouns:

| VERB | NOUN |
|---|---|
| jump | jump |
| slump | slump |
| plunge | plunge |
| gain | gain |
| improve | improvement |
| halve | half |
| lose | loss |
| strengthen | strength |

## Pronunciation

**I** and **2** 📼

**ANSWERS**

1   There was a small <u>de</u>crease in sales.
2   We im<u>port</u> some of our parts from China.
3   These cases are for <u>export</u>.
4   Have you made much <u>progress</u>?
5   We re<u>cord</u> all these transactions separately.
6   I'd like a <u>refund</u> please.

## Describing changes

**I**   Check the meanings of the phrases first if necessary, by drawing on the board the movements described in 1–6 and a–d and asking students to match the descriptions with the drawings (orally, not in writing).

Then set the labelling activity.

Don't spend too long on the vocabulary at this point as it is dealt with in 3 below.

Deal with the difference between *fell by* (the amount of the fall) and *fell to* (the point reached).

**2**   ALTERNATIVE ACTIVITY: Partners write descriptions with mistakes in, then swap, and spot their partners' mistakes.

**3**   Elicit the basic meanings — *is it large or small, fast or slow?*

**ANSWERS**

*rapid* — fast
*sharp* — large, sudden
*gradual* — small, slow
*dramatic* — very large, sudden
*negligible* — very very small, hardly noticeable

Then students explain the meaning of the words as in the examples.

**4**   Get students to define *adjective* and *adverb*, then read the introduction and try again if necessary.

**ANSWERS**

slightly, substantially, steadily, rapidly, sharply, gradually, dramatically, negligibly

SUPPLEMENTARY ACTIVITIES:

1   Dictate a graph to students using vocabulary taught/practised thus far, e.g.,

*Sales rose sharply in January, then fell steadily until June when they levelled off ...*

Students must try to draw the shapes they hear. Then draw the graph of your description on the board and ask students to compare it with their versions. Deal with problems/misunderstandings.

2   Students draw graphs, dictate them to each other, then compare graphs.

**5**   See Student's Book.

## Causes and results

**I** and **2**   Work out the cause and effect chain (Student's Book page 97) for the first trend, then let students try the others, e.g.,

Medicine is improving — People are living longer — Governments need to spend more on old people

If students have difficulty, move straight to exercise 2.

**ANSWERS**

1 d   2 e   3 a   4 g   5 c   6 b   7 f

When they have worked out most of the chains, set the sentence writing activity.

KEY LANGUAGE POINT: There are three types of cause represented in the four phrases in the box:

1   the only cause — *a result of/because of*
2   the main cause — *largely due to*
3   one of many causes — *contributed to*

**3**   This can be set for homework.

# SKILLS WORK

---
**Optional equipment and materials**
Jigsaw of activities and events exercise 2, page 104

---

## Writing

**1**  If this is a new lesson revise/remind students of the cause and effect chain.

Find first phrase as an example:

*can be attributed to*

**ANSWERS**
which led to; which resulted from; was largely due to; (was) brought about by; will lead to; and consequently

NOTE: *result in* vs. *result from*: the different preposition changes the direction of cause and effect.

Ask students to explain the meaning of vocabulary and cohesive devices:

turnaround; simplified; merchandising; margins; alliance; consequently; one of *these* (these what?); a second *factor* (in what?); *this* was largely due (what was?)

**2**  Check the form of the diagram by asking comprehension questions:

*Why are there three boxes on the right?*
(Because there were three results from activities and events according to the report.)

*Why are there three arrows to the first box?*
(Because there were three factors leading to the first result.)

**3**  The diagram has the same structure as that in 2 so the report can also have the same structure.

Look at key expressions in 1 and prepare the report with the class if necessary. Then set the activity and monitor writing.

Take in the report and mark for communicative competence first, grammatical accuracy second.

## Speaking

Write STEP on the board and elicit/teach the four adjectives. Check by taking examples from the boxes in the illustration and asking which type of change they belong to, e.g.,

**Teacher:** *computers,*
**Students:** *technological.*

Set the activity.

ALTERNATIVE ACTIVITIES:

**1**  With the students, do a STEP analysis of the school or institute in which you are working.

**2**  A student gives a mini-lecture on a STEP analysis they have done for their industry.

CLOSURE: Follow the procedure on page 11.

## PRESENTATION

**1** [cassette] Remind students of the stages in solving a problem:

define the problem
establish criteria for the solution
generate alternatives
evaluate alternatives
decide on the best alternative
inform people who need to know

Explain that they are going to listen to someone with a problem talking to a consultant. Ask students to read the first sentence of the introduction and define the problem. Then ask them to put the stages in order *before* they listen to the conversation.

Play the conversation for them to check their ideas.

**ANSWERS**
3, 5, 2, 6, 1, 4

Check vocabulary. Ask students to find the word which means:

1  what they want to do (*objective*)
2  the exact details of the machine — size, capacity, etc. (*specification*)
3  a rough drawing (*sketch*)
4  alternatives (*options*)
5  a drawing from which something can be built (*design*)

Students check the answers; they should define the words without looking at the definitions.

**2** Students can use the completed list from 1.

Highlight the verbs and deal with the passive.

KEY LANGUAGE POINT: The Passive Verb *to be* (agreeing with subject in number) + past participle.

The tense is selected on the same basis as the active form would be selected. The passive is often used where the actions are more important than the people performing them; in this case, we do not really care who identifies the design objectives.

Elicit/teach a few more 'staging' phrases, e.g.,

*And then? And after that? What next?*

Students work through the whole design process then check in pairs.

Deal with problems, especially:

verb *to be* in wrong form,
verb *to be* not agreeing with subject in number,
wrong form of main verb (*written*, *done*, *drawn* are irregular).

**3** [cassette] Give students a few moments to read the questions before playing the tape again.

**ANSWERS**
1  Reliable, efficient
2  Cooling the motor, vibration
3  When they discuss the different options
4  At least two weeks

Elicit answers and check the vocabulary, e.g.,

T: *The motor must be reliable which means ...*
S: *It mustn't break down a lot.*

*It must be efficient which means ...*
*It must have low running costs.*

*The temperature must be kept low so ...*
*We must cool it.*

*We don't want it to move a lot so ...*
*It mustn't vibrate a lot.*

Remind students of some of the words used in the conversation to express obligation. (Use the word *obligation*, as this will help later.)

**4** Tell students to use each expression once only.

Make sure they have the correct answers but don't yet explain why. Ask if they can work out the difference between:

*You must* and *You have to*
*You mustn't* and *You don't have to*

**ANSWERS**
*Must* (or *has to*)
*Don't have to*
*Must* (or *have to*)
*Mustn't*

Before going through the Key Language Points, check concepts:

*Is it necessary for the consultant to worry about dust?*

*Is it necessary for him to solve the vibration problem?*

*Is it necessary that the machine doesn't vibrate above limits?*

Then ask students to make sentences with *must/have to* for these cases.

KEY LANGUAGE POINTS:

1   There is only a slight difference in meaning between *You must* and *You have to*.

In the first person, *must* tends to express internal obligation — obligation you are imposing on yourself — whereas *have to* tends to suggest some external authority obliging you to act. However, when not used in the first person, it is doubtful whether there is any real difference.

2   The main difference between

*You mustn't* and *You don't have to*

is between imposing a negative obligation and negating the obligation, i.e.,

*It's necessary for you not to do it*
= you mustn't

*It's not necessary for you to do it*
= you don't have to

**5**  **ANSWERS**

Gap fill: *should, ought, can, be able to*
With *to: ought, be able*
Similar meanings: *should* and *ought, can* and *be able*

KEY GRAMMAR:

1   There is only a small difference between *should* and *ought to*.

In some cases there is a suggestion with *ought to* that, although an obligation is recognized, it is not going to be met, e.g.,

*I ought to write, but I'm not going to.*

But here they both represent obligation which is slightly weaker than *must*.

2   There is no difference in meaning between *can* and *be able to* in this case, but only the second is used in the future form. The future form is only used where something has to change

between now and the future time to make the activity possible, e.g.,

*I can give you them today or I can give you them tomorrow.*

but

*I can't give you them today but I'll be able to give you them tomorrow* (when I've finished them).

# LANGUAGE WORK

> **Optional equipment and materials**
>
> *for pre-experience students:*
>
> Information about a local company for exercise 5, page 113

## Pronunciation

1   [▭]   Try to get students to explain the difference in pronunciations before reading the exposition. Whether they can or not, get them to produce the three pronunciations from the phonemic script and assist as necessary.

When you have established the different pronunciations, ask

T: *So when is* can *stressed and when is it unstressed?*

Answers:

Unstressed — when it is part of a phrase including the main verb

Stressed — when the main verb is not present and/or when the ability or possibility has previously been called into question, e.g.,

A: *I thought you couldn't do it.*
B: *Well, we CAN do it* (but it will cost more.)

KEY LANGUAGE POINT: Pronouncing *can/can't*

It is difficult to hear the 'nt' cluster and sometimes impossible, e.g., *We can't tell him*. Because of this, native (British) English speakers perceive the long vowel in between /k/ and /n/ as the negative marker (*caaan go* as *can't go*).

60

For this reason it is essential that students learn to shorten the vowel in the unstressed *can* — the most common form.

**2** As in Student's Book.

## Terms of business

**I** Introduce the idea of the title of this section by pointing out that companies have rights and responsibilities in their relationships with their suppliers and customers — things they can do and things they must do. To talk about these things in English we need a large number of *modals*. Ask students if they know any modals and put any elicited on board which express obligation and ability.

**ANSWERS**
1  Necessary: *must, have to, need to, have got to*
2  Not necessary: *don't have to, needn't*
3  Good things to do: *should, ought to*
4  Bad things to do: *shouldn't, mustn't* (strong — can be a prohibition)
5  Possible: *can*
6  Impossible: *can't*

**2** Remind students what the phrase *terms of business* means and elicit terms that they use with their customers or suppliers.

**PX** Pre-experience students can think about it from the point of view of a customer.

Let students work in groups. If you know they will find it difficult, give them the answers mixed up for a matching activity.

**ANSWERS**
1  You can save money on this for a short time.
2  You don't have to/needn't pay extra for this.
3  You must/have to pay before you receive the service.
4  You can rent or buy.
5  You can't pay this way.
6  You should return it.
7  You can get your money back if you are not happy.
8  You don't have to/needn't pay extra for this if …
9  You must pay within …
10  You can have this immediately.
11  You can have this for 30 days before paying.

12  You don't have to pay for the call or the demonstration.
13  You should make out the cheque to …
14  If you don't sell this, you can return it.
15  You can get this cheaper if …

NOTE: Other methods of expressing the same information are possible.

**3** This exercise looks at how we talk about terms of business, then follow the procedure in the Student's Book.

**ANSWERS**
Ability: *could, we've been able to, couldn't*
Obligation: *they had to,*
We use *be able to* instead of *can*, e.g., *have been able to.*
We use *have to* instead of *must*, e.g., *had to.*

**4** As in Student's Book.

## Meeting requirements

**I** and **2**   See Student's Book. For pre-experience students see below.

**3** Talk generally about why customers choose one company rather than another. Do students have any idea of customers looking for 'added value' over and above the generic product? The question is *what is important to their customers* not *what do they do better than competitors.*

**4** Possible other factors: pleasant staff with a good attitude, speedy decision making, speedy response to enquiries, jargon-free sales people.

**5** See Student's Book.

SUPPLEMENTARY ACTIVITY: What do the suppliers of the students' companies have to do to meet their requirements?

**PX** ALTERNATIVE ACTIVITIES: covering activities 1–5: go straight to activity 2, but instead of talking about their company's products and services, ask students to make two lists of adjectives connected with (a) products, (b) services.

Activity 3: Ask students which things they think are important:

a   to a student thinking of joining a General English language course

b   to a person buying a new computer for his/her office

c   to an office manager who wants to buy stationery items

d   to a training officer who wants to buy specialized language courses.

Activity 4: as (4) above.

Activity 5: Students discuss what they think is important about a company when they want:

1   a product, e.g., a television
2   a service, e.g., that provided by a travel agency

## Technical description

1   As in the Student's Book, or make it into a game: Put the students in groups and give them twenty points if they can guess the item from A and ten if they need B as well; give a further five points if they give the exact word or phrase for the thing and another five if they can spell and pronounce it correctly.

**ANSWERS**
1   <u>Fire</u> ex<u>tin</u>guisher
2   <u>Photo</u>copier
3   <u>Park</u>ing <u>me</u>ter
4   Re<u>char</u>geable <u>ba</u>ttery
5   <u>Head</u>lights
6   <u>Ra</u>dio <u>mi</u>crophone

**2** **ANSWERS**

| | | | |
|---|---|---|---|
| 1 | A texts | 4 | A texts |
| 2 | B texts | 5 | A texts |
| 3 | B texts | 6 | B texts |

1   has been stored, is released, is depressed
2   was invented, is attracted
3   is moved, is raised
4   is produced, are connected
5   have been placed, are reflected
6   will be emitted

KEY LANGUAGE POINT: Refer students to the Grammar Note and ask them to think about how they do these things in their own language:

a   refer to people in general — like A
b   give technical descriptions — like B

More articulate students may be able to explain to the class, e.g.,

*We use a special form which means 'He', but which is only used in this case.*

*You* is perfectly acceptable for this 'general person' sense; the general person pronoun *one* is rather rare and is generally associated with a rather affected, upper-class language use.

The passive is common in technical description and avoids the need for any general person pronoun.

## Total Quality Management

1   Give students time to discuss the questions. Exploit the visual, e.g.,

How can you 'do it wrong first time'?

What happens if you 'stamp something out'?

Why am I responsible for quality? — I am not in the Quality Control Department.

What is the joke here? (A pun on the two meanings of 'Q'—*quality* and *queue*)

NOTE: TQM is one of a number of associated ideas which collectively replace the idea of Quality Control — largely at the end of each operational process — with Quality Assurance to achieve zero defects. If the concept is new to you point this out to your students as it will soon become apparent anyway! Students may associate it with Japan and certainly a lot of the work of the 'gurus' — Deming and Juran — is based on Japanese experiences. TQM is also associated with the idea of 'internal customers' — the idea that we all have somebody to satisfy, even if that person is also on the staff of our organization.

**2** Ask students to read the article and think about one question:

What do you have to do to achieve quality?

**ANSWERS**

1  Do it right first time
2  Don't waste resources
3  Throw out outdated processes
4  Involve everyone in the organization
5  Give employees more decision making powers
6  Support employees
7  Create teams

Ask students what they think about the ideas.

**3**  See the Student's Book.

**4  ANSWERS**

3  are made
4  have to be fixed
5  are incurred
6  is done
7  musn't be wasted
8  have to be thrown out
9  has to be involved
10  has to be pushed
11  have to be made
12  has to be stood
13  have to be given
14  should be supported
15  can't be done
16  can only be done
(Students needn't write anything for Paragraph 2.)

**5**  NOTE: Many students' companies may be engaged in international quality accreditation schemes, such as ISO 9000. Attitudes may vary, so be prepared for a long discussion on the value of such schemes.

# SKILLS WORK

**Optional equipment and materials**
Dictionaries for checking pages 116 and 117

## Speaking

**1** and **2**  See Student's Book

If possible monitor as the questions are being produced and guide/correct so that the questions are accurate before stage 2.

**PX**  As an alternative, use the scenario from the last activity of Language Work above as the basis for the questions and eventual pair work role play.

## Reading

Check comprehension with a 'Many a Slip' (see page 28):

*Speaking is an excellent way to improve your income. But it isn't sensible to look up everyone you meet in an atlas. You need to develop the habit of smoking and reading magazines. If necessary you can often guess what stories are about. This exercise gives practice in working outside.*

**1**  Explain that 'skimming' — reading to get a general idea of a topic — is an important reading skill and one they have to practise. This exercise will help. Be very strict about the time.

**2**  Monitor and note confusion or misunderstandings.

**3**  Do a general check on narrative comprehension before checking detailed vocabulary comprehension. Then give students some language to discuss possible meanings of italicized items:

*It must be    a(n) adjective/verb/noun
                a kind of ...
                something to do with*

Do the first two or three with them to give them the idea.

NOTE: GUESSING UNKNOWN WORDS (Student's Book page 116) deals with the points raised by these words.

**4** Check the main points of the story — that the business started because a person needed something himself and invented a better product than those on the market. Perhaps it is also important that the inventor was very young and the product now has international sales. Then ask students if they have similar stories — you might preview this at the end of one lesson for telling at the beginning of the next.

GUESSING UNKNOWN WORDS: See Student's Book. As a further step towards student autonomy, let them use a dictionary to find the answers, or check with each other in large groups.

CLOSURE: Follow the procedure on page 11.

# 12 Comparing Options

## PRESENTATION

1 Give students time to answer the question then elicit answers. Tell them you have a very full answer and that they must get all the information. Push them until they produce something like:

*It is an estimate of the costs of printing 50,000 four colour catalogues in either Hong Kong or Europe.*

If students are really struggling, prompt with a series of questions:

*Is it an invoice?*
*What kind of work is it for?*
*How many?*
*Where?*

Check the 'Hong Kong or Europe' part by asking:

*What are the two kinds of costs shown?*
*Why are the first four costs fixed?*
*Why are the next two costs variable?*
*Which option is cheaper?*

### POSSIBLE ANSWERS
Fixed costs are the same wherever the catalogue is printed — perhaps these activities are going to be done in the UK.

Variable costs are different (vary), depending on where the catalogues are printed.

2 Be prepared to play sections of the tape again if there are any problems. If students routinely bring calculators ask them to check the figures as this is also a comprehension check. (In fact, the cost per copy in HK is 2.52 so see if anyone spots that!)

### ANSWERS
*extent*: 368 pages
*freight*: HK 3,500 pounds; Europe 1,000 pounds
*delivery*: HK 6 weeks; Europe 2 weeks
*exchange rate*: 1 pound = 11 HK$
*per copy*: HK 2.51 pounds; Europe 2.70 pounds

SUPPLEMENTARY ACTIVITIES:
1 If students are still struggling with hearing or producing numbers, do more work on the numbers, e.g.,

a Students check all the addition — 9,200 + 1,840 = etc.
b Dictate a changed estimate — composition and proofs has gone up to 9,234, etc.
c Ask them to make savings on some of the items of 10% and recalculate the cost.
d Ask them to recalculate the costs if you ordered 100,000.

2 Ask students to summarize the print estimate in one sentence, e.g., *Hong Kong is much cheaper at the current rate of exchange but delivery time is much longer.*

3 Ask students to explain any differences between these words used in the conversation: *bill, price, estimate, costing, costs, rate, figure.*

## 3 ANSWERS
1 If
2 in case
3 until
4 when
5 unless

Ask students to explain why all the sentences in this exercise are similar. (Two ideas for the future are linked by a word or phrase which tells you more about the relationship between the two ideas.)

## Pronunciation

1 Practise saying the linked words. Show how the last consonant seems to attach to the next word thus:

wha - tabout; hea - doffice

## 2 ANSWERS
1 same as
2 have a
3 There's another
4 calculated on, basis of
5 work out, out at

Practise saying the linked words, then the whole sentence.

**3** 🔲 As in Student's Book.

Let students read introduction. Go through the example and the closing sentence. Elicit the information that a consonant sound is added – a /w/ after /o/ a /j/ after /i:/.

**4** 🔲 **ANSWERS**

1  I've    used  a rate  of ... to    eleven
          /j/                        /w/

2  On the       other ... that's   only   a ... part   of
          /j/


# LANGUAGE WORK


## Comparing products


**1**  Let students read the introduction then check the scenario by asking quick questions.

*What in this case is 'a fleet'?*
*What do you need to buy?*
*What are the options?*
*What have you got to do with the statements?*

No right or wrong answers to the statements at this stage, of course!

**2**  When you go through the students' answers make sure students can tell you why answers were true or false.

**ANSWERS**

| | | |
|---|---|---|
| 1 | *False* | see list prices of equivalent models |
| 2 | *True* | see running cost of equivalent models and 'diesels (are) much more economical to run' |
| 3 | *True* | 'times have changed/more and more people ...' |
| 4 | *True* | 'over the lifetime ... Worked out far cheaper' |
| 5 | *False* | 'the modern diesel can match the performance..' |
| 6 | *False* | 'the exhaust ... Is as clean as ... ' |

If students are still struggling, do further work on the table. Check the column headings by asking students to cover them and recall what they were. Deal with any problems such as:

1  *Make* vs. *model* (*Make* = manufacturer; *model* = type)

2  Are there any other *fuels*? (Alcohol or gas for cars; kerosene for aircraft; and (not for cars) coal, oil etc.)

3  Why *list* price? (Because the selling price might be discounted)

4  What is involved in *running costs*? (Fuel and repairs/service)

5  What exactly does the last column heading mean? (How much you save with diesel over three years or 60,000 miles)

SUPPLEMENTARY ACTIVITY: Ask students to find the word in the article which means:

1  what people say about something or someone (*reputation*)

2  cars, buses, lorries, etc. (*vehicle*)

3  things or people of the same type (*counterparts*)

4  with poor acceleration (*sluggish*)

5  how well the engine goes, especially how fast (*performance*)

6  the good things (*benefits*)

7  not containing (*-free*)

8  a large number of vehicles (*fleet*)

**3**  Activity 1: Students do the underlining. Write the phrases onto the board so you can isolate and group the different elements in the following activities. Students work out answers to (a), (b), and (c). Give further examples in the case of (a) and (b) to guide students to the correct answer.

**ANSWERS**

cheaper ... than/more expensive ... than;

fewer people ... than/less money than;

is better (than the performance ...)/is worse (than pollution ...);

**a**  one syllable = + -er;
two syllables = sometimes +-er; sometimes *more*;
more than two syllables = *more*

**b**  *fewer* with countable, *less* with uncountable

**c**  *better, worse*

Activity 2: Refer students to the article.

**ANSWERS**
*Much (more economical)* or *far (cheaper)*

Activity 3:
**ANSWERS**
The Audi 100D 2.5 is the most expensive.
The Rover 800 2.0 is the cheapest.
Comparatives for two things; superlatives for three or more.

**4**  Give students a few moments to think of some questions before putting them in pairs. Monitor and get students to repeat good questions at the end of the pairwork.

POSSIBLE QUESTIONS: Which car – is the most economical? (see 'Cost per mile')

– has the longest range? (see 'Tank' and 'Fuel consumption')

– has the best performance? (see 'Maximum speed' and '0-60 mph')

– has the most added value? (see 'What the price includes')

– is the best value for money? (for a company fleet — any reasonable ideas)

**5**  See Student's Book.

## Interpreting statistics

If some or all of your students have not covered graphs and tables in previous lessons, spend some time getting students to identify the following on each graph:

the vertical scale

the horizontal scale

what the graph represents — the subject

what the graph shows — what you can tell from it

particular statistics which can be read from the graph.

In the case of a tables check:

*   column headings
*   row headings
*   what it represents
*   what it shows
*   particular statistics

You could also do a speed quiz with questions like:

1   What is the life expectancy in Japan?

2   What percentage of Spaniards have a telephone?

3   Which country has the highest number of doctors per million people?

**1**  Elicit observations from students — one each, if time permits.

**2**  If your students will find the procedures in the Student's Book too challenging, ask them to base their judgements only on the graphs and tables. But be careful with a multilingual group whose nationalities are represented in the tables. You do not want the discussion to become acrimonious!

## Moral standards

Think carefully about how your students will react to the information and the questions on this page. **Don't do the activities if you think they might offend.**

**1**  It will be easier to 'explain' *moral standards* and *civic morality* after you have looked at some of the information. Ask students to try to explain the illustration. General discussion on the questions in 1, then students read the article. You might like to set some 'while reading' activities:

*Which continent is the article talking about?*
*How many people were surveyed?*
*How many countries were involved?*
*What were the questions about?*
*Why might these results not be accurate?*

Ask what *moral* standards means.
Explain that *civic* means related to society.
Ask what *civic morality* means.

**2 and 3**  Before starting, check that students understand that the numbers on the chart show the rank order on each issue: 1 = most moral / honest. Ask about a few issues, e.g.,

*Which country scores best on dropping litter in the street?*

Ask about a few countries, e.g.,

*What does Britain score best on?*

67

Explain how the position of Norway is arrived at:

*Norway is near the top on all issues except ... therefore ...*

**4** Ask students to answer the questions themselves then widen it to a general discussion.

VOCABULARY NOTE: *Anti*social means against — society its norms and traditions. *Un*social means not social — at a strange time of day; for example, *He works unsocial hours.*

**5** ANSWERS

| | | |
|---|---|---|
| unjustified | immoral | dishonest |
| illegal | irresponsible | inaccurate |

There are no vocabulary rules for using, e.g., *un-* or *in-* as a negative prefix, but there are some phonological rules for changing the spelling of *in-*.

Ask students to work them out from the examples. Elicit/add some more if they are struggling: *immoral\**, *illegal*, *irresponsible*, *inaccurate*.

Other examples: *impossible, illiterate, irregular, inappropriate.*

Words beginning with *m* or *p*: change *in-* to *im-*.

Words beginning with *r*: change *in-* to *-ir*.

Words beginning with *l*: change *in-* to *il-*.

Others remain *in-*.

\*NOTE: *immoral* means not moral, breaking the moral code; *amoral* means not having a moral code at all.

**6** Remind students that some words in the exercise may use *un-* or *dis-* to form the opposite.

ANSWERS

| | | |
|---|---|---|
| unfair | incorrect | impossible |
| impolite | irregular | inconvenient |
| irrelevant | illogical | unreliable |
| disorganized | inefficient | impractical |
| unlikely | uncertain | improbable |

NOTE: *Disorganized* = in a mess; *unorganized* = not organized

## Business ethics

Do not worry about new vocabulary while students are doing the quiz. Remind them of techniques they have learnt for guessing the meaning of new words (Student's Book pages 116–17).

If necessary, check understanding the scenarios with the whole class before going into groups to choose answers. Do not, at this stage, go into the 'moral issue'.

Students check — and try to understand — how they scored. Ask if they agree with the interpretation of their score.

If you have time, get the students to tell you each scenario and, this time, to explain the moral issue, e.g.,

**1** You have free flight vouchers which really belong to your company because they paid for the air travel. Give students time to argue the case for or against each course of action.

## Contingency Plans

**1** Explain the title — it is planning for things which might happen, usually things which might go wrong. Remind students of the structure of the 1st conditional and the meaning — the speaker thinks the event is quite likely. Check for the correct form of all verbs.

**2** ANSWERS

**1** In the first sentence, the decision as to whether to hire the interpreter depends on whether or not she speaks English; in the second sentence, the decision to hire the interpreter has already been taken (as a precaution).

**2** With *if* it's not certain that the designer will be free, whereas with *when* it is certain.

**3** In the first sentence, the implication is that she has already seen the plans and so will only need to see them again if they've been changed. In the second sentence, *unless* = *if not*; the implication is that the changes will prevent him from showing her the plans.

**4** In the first sentence, she doesn't want the contract to be altered; in the second sentence she does want it altered.

KEY LANGUAGE POINT: *Unless* can also be used to introduce negative conditions where *if not* could not be substituted, e.g.,

*Don't ask me unless you can't find it in a dictionary.*

We could, of course, strip out both negatives and replace them with: *Don't ask me if you can find it.*

Here *until* means 'from now to an unspecified time when an event may or may not happen'. *Until* also means 'from this time to this time', e.g., *from 1991 to 2004.*

**3** This activity is the proof of understanding the previous one. If necessary, get the class back together to re-teach items which are still causing confusion.

NOTE: The conditionals used here are open — in other words, there is no fixed format to the tenses as there is in 1st and 2nd conditionals (covered in previous units).

Possible mixed tenses could be:

*Don't leave anything valuable in case it is stolen.*

*It's best to go on foot unless you would prefer to drive.*

# SKILLS WORK

## Speaking

Remind students of the 'generating alternatives' stage in problem solving. Ask for the best way to get a number of alternative solutions to a problem. (Probably, the best way is brainstorming.)

**I** If students are not sure about the word *motivation* , let them read on to the second paragraph and look at the three example ideas. Then get them to explain the word to you. If students are stuck, be prepared to add some ideas:

more challenging work
praise and encouragement
clear targets
training courses
suggestion schemes

profit-related bonuses
competitions and prizes

ALTERNATIVE FOR LARGE CLASSES: divide students into groups and let them appoint a scribe and brainstorm. Then ask the scribe to report back and get a composite list on the board. If necessary, help appoint the 'scribe' and give him/her process language to use:

*How can I say that in one sentence?*
*What exactly shall I write?*
*So can you put that in a few words?*

**2** NOTE: Remind students that evaluating alternatives is a good idea before worrying about implementation. If then you decide on the most effective way to solve a problem, you should certainly try to find a way to implement it.

**3** and **4**   Report back and discuss as a class.

**5**   See Student's Book.

Further questions to stimulate discussion:

*Are managers and workers motivated by the same things?*

*Are staff motivated in your company? Why (not)?*

## Listening

**I** Check comprehension of the background information, perhaps with 'Many a Slip':

*Steve Copper is one of the least distinguished managers in English handball. For ninety years he managed Buckingham Palace football team and during that time he failed to transform them into a highly expensive premier division front.*

Then follow the Student's Book.

**2**   ▭   Spend some time discussing areas of disagreement between Coppell's views and the students'.

   **ANSWERS**
   **I**   He probably would agree — he bought a pool table and fruit machines presumably so they had somewhere to spend time together, but he does actually say 'when players choose to spend time together ...' so he clearly doesn't believe in forcing.

69

**2** He wouldn't agree.
**3** He would agree.
**4** He would agree.
**5** He wouldn't agree.

**3**  ▭  Give students a chance to think about the endings before playing the tape again. Be prepared to play the tape sections several times to give students a chance to complete them accurately.

**ANSWERS**
**I** it generates a better atmosphere.
**2** I can guarantee they won't play well.
**3** then I'm incompetent if I keep on employing them.
**4** then I should leave them alone to get on with it.
**5** I don't feel I have to explain it to them.
**6** I'll say 'come back and talk about it in a couple of days' time'.
**7** I won't waste my time on them.

CLOSURE: Follow the procedure on page 11.

# PRESENTATION

**1**   Ask students to read the introduction and to make notes as they listen to help them answer the questions at the end. Play Part 1.

### ANSWERS

They can't produce the new design. The problem arose when the designer moved a socket.

**2**    **ANSWERS**

changed the design – D/E
incorporated a smaller battery – D
moved a socket – D
couldn't meet the new specifications – E
built the prototype – E
didn't check – D/E

Elicit possible endings for the sentence then highlight the grammar of the example:

| They didn't check ... | **so** we didn't avoid ... |
|---|---|
| **but** | |
| If they had checked... we would have avoided... | |
| past perfect | *would* + *have* + past participle |

**3**   Ask students what they think the managers should do next.

Then tell them to listen and find out what options the managers considered.

After they have listened, ask individual students to suggest the two options and any advantages or disadvantages they heard, but don't let them write anything.

**4**   You may have to play the tape again. If possible, monitor to see how good the students' responses are before writing them into a matrix on the board.

### ANSWERS

| Options | Advantages | Disadvantages |
|---|---|---|
| **1** Go back to the drawing board | Would meet specifications | Would lose time |
| **2** Play about with the existing designs | Would save time | Would have to accept a lower quality product |

**5** Point out the form of the modals in the advantages and disadvantages columns. Ask why they are in this form. (Because the speakers think both options are unlikely — perhaps because it is such a difficult problem to solve.) Highlight the grammar in the example and then give students time to work out three more from the table.

### ANSWERS

If we went back to the drawing board, we would be able to meet the specifications.

If we went back to the drawing board, we would lose time.

If we played about with the existing designs, we would save time.

If we played about with the existing designs, we would have to accept a lower quality product.

VOCABULARY NOTE: During this section it is likely that students have been quoting from the meeting. This could give you a lead-in to the note. You could even do it as a discovery learning activity if you asked students to invent some rules and then gave the examples here for them to confirm or correct their rules.

## Pronunciation  ▭

Get students to explain the difference as well as choose the different one. If students are struggling, be prepared to re-teach the sounds, and do some ear training, e.g.,

T:  When I say /ɪ/, you say 1;
    when I say /iː/, you say 2.
    Now listen: /iː/, /iː/, /ɪ/, /iː/) *me, meet, it, eat*, etc.

**ANSWERS AND NOTES**
1  *it* — short vowel /ɪ/, not long /iː/
2  *said* — short /e/ not diphthong /eɪ/
3  *draw* — /ɔː/ not /ɜː/
4  *feel* — long vowel /iː/, not short /ɪ/
5  *they* — diphthong /eɪ/ not short vowel /ɪ/
6  *word* — /ɜː/ not /ɔː/

# LANGUAGE WORK

### Checking understanding

In general people do not check they understand enough even in their first language. In addition, being prepared to interrupt – if it is culturally acceptable — and ask checking questions, ensures that people are listening actively – another thing people don't do at meetings even in their own language!

1  Work through the introduction down to the example sentence. Then elicit as many responses as possible before going on to the ones printed in the Student's Book and setting the exercise. Draw students attention to the note under the meanings a–e.

**POSSIBLE ANSWERS**
a  6, 8
b  1, 5
c  2, 7
d  4
e  3, 9

2  Practise some of the phrases chorally and individually. Choose a few students and give them time to prepare a one minute talk on one of the subjects listed, dealing with any problems with the titles. Student's deliver their mini-lectures whilst the rest of the class interrupt. If you prefer, make it a game and award points to interruptions. Keep it light-hearted!

3  Explain that when we don't understand what someone said, it helps to be exact, so we should explain precisely what it is we *haven't* understood. Ask the students to read the example and then get the three possible meanings on the board as a diagram plus the alternative ways of checking. Practise the sentences in the example.

Then work through 1 together, eliciting alternative meanings — see the board plan.

At the end of the pairwork, get possible interpretations of each phrase on the board. In the process you will develop useful language and broaden some students' horizons on possible interpretations.

| e.g., **Reduce staffing costs** | | |
|---|---|---|
| not replace staff who should resign | cut wages? | make staff redundant? |
| *Do you mean?* | *Are you saying...?* | *Are you suggesting...?* |
| **1   improve the level of English** | | |
| employ people who speak English? | train existing staff? | sack people who don't speak English? |

4  Ask students to summarize what they have done so far this lesson/this week/this month. Then let them read the introduction. Do one of the topics as an example, giving a point in favour and one against and asking a good student to summarize your views.

Give some language for the students to introduce the summary:

*So you're saying...*
*So you think...*
*So in your opinion...*

Then put them in pairs to complete the task. Monitor and identify some cases where the summary was not completely accurate. If the speaker corrected this, get them to do so again as an open pair in front of the class. Otherwise give some language for correcting inaccurate summaries:

*Well, I don't mean ...*
*Actually, I didn't say ...*
*That's not quite what I meant.*

## Expressing opinions

1 Remind students that at meetings this type of conversation happens frequently:

Speaker A: Proposal + Justification
Speaker B: Rejection

E.g.,
A: In my opinion we should reduce the temperature of the workshops by two degrees. That would save a lot of money on heating bills.

B: I'm not sure. It would cause disputes with the union.

Highlight the uses of the *would* form, and the way it is said in connected speech.

### ANSWERS

| **a** to justify: | **b** to reject: |
|---|---|
| *It'd save money...* | *It'd be risky.* |
| *It'd mean we could...* | *It wouldn't be cost effective.* |
| *It'd enable us to...* | *It wouldn't be right.* |
| *It'd save time.* | *It'd be very short-sighted.* |
| *It'd improve...* | *It'd cause disputes.* |

SUPPLEMENTARY ACTIVITY: Check that the justifications and rejections are understood by giving some headwords and asking students to match phrases used in exercise 1 to the headwords. For example, a speaker might justify or reject a proposal on financial grounds: It'd save money; It wouldn't be cost effective. Headwords:

| | |
|---|---|
| *finance* | *labour relations* |
| *threat/opportunity* | *quality* |
| *ethics* | *strategy* |

Ask students to add some more headwords of the same sort.

2 See Student's Book.

3 Remind students that the main role of many meetings is to get a wide range of opinions and ideas — the '*generate alternatives* stage' of problem solving. Try to elicit phrases for collecting other people's opinions then go to examples.

Practise these chorally and individually. Then go into the role play.

NOTE: You may have to deal here with the difference between:

What do you *mean*? (= I don't understand.)
What do you *think*? (= What's your opinion?)

ROLE PLAY: Give students plenty of time to come to terms with the general scenario, their role and the information available to them in the files. Some of the vocabulary — e.g., one-armed bandit — should be new to others at the meeting to encourage students to check their understanding. But, since all the directors work for the same company, it is reasonable to suppose that some words will be common currency: deal with some of these as a whole group before asking students to look at their individual files. Possible general words: *ingredients*, *cartons*, *tins*, *rest room*, *pack* (verb). During the role play, keep a very low profile, but prompt individuals if necessary.

LESSON PLANNING NOTE: If this is the end of a lesson, set activity 5 on the next page for homework — not writing, just thinking about it.

## Hypothesizing

1 When students have completed the activity go back to the word *hypothetical* and ask what it means (not true/not factual)

### ANSWERS

1 Past situation that didn't happen — past perfect, past conditional — called the third conditional

2 Future situation unlikely to happen — past, conditional — called the second conditional

Show the connection between: hyp<u>o</u>thesize (verb), hyp<u>o</u>thesis (noun), and hyp<u>o</u>th<u>e</u>tical (adjective). Practise pronunciation and stress.

KEY LANGUAGE POINT: Remember that in some languages, the equivalent of the conditional is on both sides of the sentence — the *if* clause and the other one. So some students will have to resist the temptation to put ~~If I would~~...

73

**2** Do the first one or two to check students understand the activity and/or use example for 3 below to illustrate. With an outgoing group, give them 30 seconds to consider each sentence then ask several students for endings. Skip 3 below. With more reserved students, allow more time — even overnight — for them to think about the endings and possibly write them down. Then go on to 3.

**3** See Student's Book.

**4** We often hypothesize about the past when we feel the past could have been better – if only we'd known! Work through the grammatical changes and drill some of them if necessary, e.g.,

*You didn't know...*    —    *If I'd known...*
*so you took...*        —    *I wouldn't have taken...*
*You didn't know...*
*so you went...*
*She didn't give you...*
*so you had to...*

If students are struggling, isolate the verbs and drill infinitive/past/past participle first, e.g., *know — knew, known; take — took, taken.*

Irregular verbs here are:

*know, go, give, have to, be, take, tell, buy, think, beat*

Then try the more complete drill again. Ask students to make sentences as per examples.

**5** If possible, give the students time to think about this: set it the lesson before, for example.

# SKILLS WORK

> **Optional equipment and materials**
> Jigsaw of stories in exercise 1, page 136

## Reading

**1** Remind students that before they read anything they should think about what they are going to read. Who wrote it? What information can they learn from it? For example, people look at the writing on envelopes and the postmark before opening a letter.

People have a purpose in mind before opening a telephone directory.

Ask them to read the introduction — the first two sentences — but first, ask them what information they can learn from it.

After they have read the opening extracts, ask what information they can learn from the stories. (The mistakes the managers made, and what they learnt from them.) Finally, ask what structure they expect to find in stories of this kind — how will they begin, what will be in the middle part, how will they end. (Possible answers: BEGINNING — scene setting — *was doing / had done*; MIDDLE — narrative — *did, did, did*; END — conclusion — *if I had*; *should(n't) have done*.)

Explain that this will help them sort out the jigsaw pieces of the stories.

But first — who wrote the stories?

**ANSWERS**
Dick:   a, d, e, g, i
Lynda:  b, c, f, h, j

Ask half the class to read the biography of Lynda and the other half the biography of Dick. Then get them to tell each other the main points about Dick and Lynda's careers.

**2** ANSWERS

|                          | LKT | DB |
|--------------------------|-----|----|
| The background           | j   | d  |
| An arrangement           | h   | i  |
| What happened            | b   | g  |
| What they had to do      | f   | a  |
| What they should have done | c | e  |

**3** Let students read all the information about the activity. Then remind them of the structure of the two stories they have read. Suggest that they try to fit their story into the same structure.

NOTE: This activity could be set for a later lesson to give preparation time.

**4** Depending on your teaching style and your students' preferred learning style, either:

a   give them time to read the Grammar Notes then do activity 4

b   do activity 4, give them time to consider possible rules then refer them to the Grammar Note to check.

**ANSWERS**

| **Make** | **Do** |
|---|---|
| an offer | someone a favour |
| a phone call | a lot of damage |
| a complaint | research |
| progress | anything you like |
| a profit | your English homework |
| an appointment | your best |
| an effort | |
| a decision | |

Suggest that students write expressions with *make* and *do* in their vocabulary notebook and test themselves regularly.

**5** If students find the conversations too difficult, let them create simple sentences using the expressions in activity 4 above. Alternatively, turn it into a game where students win points for the number of times they can use *make* or *do* in one sentence.

## Speaking

GENERAL NOTE: Make sure you have plenty of time before starting activities 1–9 as they should all be done in the same lesson. Get students to use language learnt in this unit to find out exactly what the introduction means, e.g.,

T:  *Your government ...*

S:  *Sorry — do you mean the government of my country or a hypothetical country?*

T:  *Either. Your government is deregulating ...*

S:  *What does 'deregulating' mean?*

Get students to draw up an agenda for the meeting based on the nine activities on this page. In order to do this they will have to skim read everything and then decide what the basic point is in each case and how to write that on an agenda. Elicit the students' ideas and get an agreed agenda on the board. In passing deal with the fact that agendas use nouns.

> **Possible agenda**
> 1   Objective of new venture
> 2   Company image
> 3   Classes of travel
> 4   Services
> 5   In-flight entertainment
> 6   Smoking
> 7   National identity on board
> 8   Company name
> 9   Problems and solutions

It is good business practice for participants to come briefed on agenda topics so you are going to give them time to look through the nine topics. It is also common for one person to make specific proposals on each point, and for there to be a chair and a secretary — who must ask for clarifications where necessary. So you need: speakers for each topic, a chair, a secretary. If you have less than nine students, double up on topics and roles of chair and secretary. If you have more than twelve students, double up on speakers for each topic and have two secretaries.

Make sure that decisions are reached, people are put in charge of implementing the decisions, and a timescale for implementation is agreed, e.g.,

1   *We agreed that we want to achieve a large market share. Marcello is going to find out which other airlines are bidding for routes and report back at our meeting next week.*

Get the secretary to write up the minutes — with help from the rest of the class if feasible — and present them to the class as soon as possible.

ALTERNATIVE ACTIVITY FOR ONE-TO-ONE STUDENTS: If you feel that to do all these topics the preparation might be excessive, let the student choose one or two to prepare and meet to discuss just those. The student should take notes and write them up as minutes.

CLOSURE: Follow the procedure on page 11.

# PRESENTATION

> **Optional equipment and materials**
> different types of newspapers for the
> introduction to the lesson

Explain that the aim of this unit is to help make and understand business presentations — the special kind of meeting, or part of a meeting, where one person describes a project or product, or introduces their company. The presentation that students are going to hear first is connected with newspapers.

VOCABULARY BRAINSTORM: What is the common abbreviation for newspapers? – *papers*

There are four ways of classifying newspapers. Can you give the alternatives in any of these categories?

- by size (small = *tabloid*, large = *broadsheet*)

- by content (*quality* or *popular* — sometimes *heavy* or *light*)

- by distribution (*national, regional, local*)

- by time of publication (*daily, weekly, Sunday, morning, evening*)

NOTE: In Britain and some other countries, 'free' papers — papers paid for by the advertisers not the readers — have become popular in recent years. So another way of categorizing might be *paid for* or *free*.

**1** In the case of the last question, the only acceptable answer must be that it depends on what you are advertising, and who your target market is.

**2** Get students to paraphrase the introduction and instructions and double check by asking:

*She's from a market research company — so what do you think she is going to talk about?*
(surveys, questionnaires, preferences, percentages, socio-economic groups ...)

*And are you listening for one type of newspaper or two?* (two — most widely read and recommended)

Play the tape straight through once. Elicit answers and if necessary replay sections of the tape with the key information.

**ANSWERS**
A national daily tabloid.
A weekly, regional, paid-for paper.

**3** Make sure students understand how the table works — i.e., organized by time of publication first, then type, and then distribution. See if they can remember any of the missing information, then play the tape again to check/complete.

**ANSWERS**

| | |
|---|---|
| Daily national tabloid | 65% |
| Sunday national tabloid | 51% |
| Weekly regional paid-for | 8% |
| Age group 45–54 | 13% |
| Socio-economic group AB | 12% |

Ask why she recommends a newspaper with such a low figure. (Because more of their target market read that kind of paper and there is no point in advertising in papers that attract the wrong group.)

**4** When you have checked the answers, deal briefly with the grammar of the answers to Part 1 and the vocabulary of the answers to Part 2.

**ANSWERS**
Part 1: much, little, few, many, under
Part 2: recommend, advise, suggest

# LANGUAGE WORK

---
**Optional equipment and materials**

OHTs of presentation structure for exercise 3, page 142 and sentence cards for supplementary activity

Blank OHTs for students to use in exercise 4, page 142

Postcards for writing notes in mini presentations, page 145

---

## Signposting talks

In giving presentations you have to read aloud so speaking from notes is a necessary skill for business English students to acquire. However, as far as you can, you should only use notes as signposts to remind you what you are going to say.

**I** Ask students to read the introduction then check comprehension:

*What do presenters often do?*
*Why?*
*How?*

After students have underlined the phrases, ask them to make some notes on the structure of the talk.

**ANSWERS**
Phrases:
I'm going to be talking about ...
I'd like to begin by looking at ...
Then I'll move on to ...
with particular reference to ... and ...
I'll be happy to answer them as we go along.

Look back at the phrases and ask students if they can think of any more. Then go on to 2 which contains several more.

**2 ANSWERS**
I'm here to tell you a little about ...
I'd like to start by considering ...
Then I'll turn to ...
first looking at ...
and then ...
I'll do my best to answer them at the end.

**3** Ask half the class (A) to prepare the first presentation and half (B) to prepare the second. Give assistance to each half with the new or unfamiliar vocabulary. Suggest that they only use the OHT notes to guide them, rather than writing out the whole introduction. This will reduce to a minimum the amount of reading aloud.

Then, pairs of A and B students introduce their subject to their partner whilst their partner makes notes on the structure of the talk. At the end, compare the notes to the original OHTs and discuss any differences.

**4** Once again, suggest students produce notes only, not a complete script which must be read aloud verbatim. As above, judge the success of the introduction by the clarity of the notes taken by the listeners and their similarity to the notes made by the speaker.

## Pronunciation

**I** ⊡ Ask students to mark what happens to the speaker's intonation at each pause and then explain why at the end. (Rising intonation where the sentence is still continuing; falling intonation at the full stop.)

**2** Ask students to read the two example passages and the notes. Then ask why the pauses in the second are more logical than in the first. (In the first, pauses break up fixed expressions, separate adjectives from nouns, miss a full stop, and break up a verb. In the second one, pauses come after verbs, at the end of sentences, after linking words, before prepositional phrases, and before conjunctions.)

**3** ⊡ **ANSWERS**

| | |
|---|---|
| <u>gen</u>tlemen | moderni<u>za</u>tion |
| <u>con</u>ference | <u>da</u>ta-processing |
| <u>pro</u>gramme | auto<u>ma</u>tion |
| <u>cap</u>ital | par<u>tic</u>ular |
| ex<u>pen</u>diture | <u>ref</u>erence |

**4** Remind students that intonation and pausing is spoken punctuation so the pauses need to reflect the punctuation in a written version. Give students time to add the pause marks and punctuation and then play the tape for them to check.

**▭ ANSWER**

Good afternoon everyone./As you know,/I'm here to tell you about/British Telecom's/video conferencing facilities./I'd like to start by explaining/how video conferences work./Then I'll turn/to our facilities in the UK/ – first/our existing locations/then/the planned new ones./If you have any questions,/I'll do my best to answer them/ at the end.

NOTE: In real speech, pausing is often highly variable, and in practice the way in which different speakers pause does not always follow pre-determined rules. You should therefore point out to students that the version on the tape is definitely not the only 'correct' one. The important thing, when speaking a second language, is to ensure that inappropriate pauses don't make comprehension unnecessarily difficult.

**5 ▭ ANSWERS**

| | |
|---|---|
| after<u>noon</u> | fa<u>ci</u>lities |
| <u>Tel</u>ecom's | ex<u>plain</u>ing |
| <u>vi</u>deo | ex<u>ist</u>ing |
| <u>con</u>ferencing | lo<u>ca</u>tions |

## Making recommendations

Remind students that the consultant in the first part of the unit recommended where to advertise. Try to elicit that recommendation and the reason for it. (She recommended advertising in regional paid-for newspapers because more of their target market read that kind of newspaper.)

Take the two parts and turn them round. Ask the students how they could join them. Elicit or teach *so*. Add *so* to the pair of sentences to join them.

**1** Ask students to cover the endings column and try to guess what kind of recommendation might follow. Then let them uncover and complete the activity.

**ANSWERS**
1 e  2 b  3 c  4 d  5 f  6 a

NOTE: Vocabulary is practised in the supplementary activity below.

**2** Before proceeding see if students can suggest what kind of people gave the advice in any of the cases in 1. After a few attempts, refer them to the professions in 2 to complete the activity.

**ANSWERS**
1  quality consultant
2  stockbroker
3  lawyer
4  market research consultant
5  language trainer
6  travel agent

SUPPLEMENTARY ACTIVITY: Ask students to:

**1**  complete these nouns:

| | |
|---|---|
| indust(ry) | confer(ence) |
| wast(age) | automa(tion) |
| recess(ion) | refer(ence) |
| compon(ent) | facili(ties) |
| agree(ment) | moderniz(ation) |
| franch(ise) | royal(ty) |
| expendi(ture) | loc(ation) |

**2**  complete these people:

| | |
|---|---|
| ag(ent) | advis(er) |
| law(yer) | brok(er) |
| research(er) | train (er) |
| consult(ant) | deleg(ate) |

**3** This activity contains some patterns with verbs from 1 above and introduces some wrong patterns.

**ANSWERS**
Wrong patterns: 2, 4, 6

1  Get students to find the different patterns in 1.
2  Select possible patterns from this section.
3  Make a composite list of possible patterns.

Check by getting students to fill in the matrix — see the matrix below, which you can either create on the board or project with OHP.

| VERBS | | | POSSIBLE PATTERNS |
|---|---|---|---|
| **recommend** | **advise** | **suggest** | |
| √ | | √ | your (not) doing this (that) you (don't) do this |
| √ | √ | | you (not) to do this |
| √ | √ | √ | (not) doing this |
| √ | | √ | this |
| | √ | | against (doing) this |

**4** Students use the matrix as a guide to complete the sentences. Do the first one or two with them then let them continue on their own. Give them time at the end to compare answers.

**5** General discussion

**PX** Alternative questions for pre-experience students:

*Are you good at giving advice?*
*Are you good at taking advice?*
*How can you get people to accept your advice?*

## Mini presentations

**1** General discussion. If you like, make a note of people who share the same fears and put them into groups for the preparation rather than grouping on subject chosen. Remind students at this stage that they will be mini presentations — not full lectures. They must only speak for three to five minutes.

**2** **PX** These additional subjects could be used with pre-experience students.

*Why I want to be a ...*
*The biggest problem facing my country/city/region at the moment.*
*What my country must do to improve its position in world trade.*

**3** Put people into subject groups or possible skill groups (see 5 above). Give out postcards for students to write notes on if possible. Assist in the preparation as necessary. Do not give too long for preparation as this will encourage overlong presentations and raise anxiety.

**4** Give the listeners a scenario to encourage active listening, e.g., *You are going to report back on this presentation to your own company or write it up for a magazine.*

Alternatively — and choose your group carefully for this alternative — refer students to the self-study task box below in the Student's Book and get them to grade each other on these categories.

The categories are also the ones you should use for any feedback (individual or group) which you do on

the presentation. Remember: in the real business world it is the structure and organization which will impress people, provided the pronunciation, grammar, and fluency don't impede the communication. So give more weight to the first items.

## SKILLS WORK

### Reading

**1** Ask students to look at the illustration and say what they think it means. What will the article say?

Get students to answer the question in the introduction for themselves before reading the article. Prompt by asking:

*Do you have access to a computer yourself?*
*Do you use it for routine work — like word-processing — or to analyse the market and your margins, etc.?*
*Do you think computers could be used more effectively in your company?*
*If so, what is preventing this?*

Now set the reading activity — find out if they are typical.

Elicit general impressions, e.g.,

*Yes, it's the same in my company.*

Activities 2 and 3 further exploit the text.

**PX** Alternative presentation for pre-experience students:

*Do you use a computer for word-processing only or for other things as well?*
*Are computers used in your school?*
*Do you think they could be used more effectively?*

When you set the reading activity ask:

*What about computers at work in your country?*
*Do you think the findings about the USA would also be true for your country?*

SUPPLEMENTARY ACTIVITY: Ask the students how many words they can find in the text directly connected with computers. (*Software, screens, keyboards, IT, PCs, networks, applications, systems, automate, document, edit.*)

**2** Ensure that students can convert percentages into phrases such as *Most ...* which are more common in the body of a text.

Elicit/teach some introductory verbs for the comments, e.g.,

*Most of the managers said/thought/felt/ commented...*

**3** Ask students to find the information in the text and then make notes in two columns.

**4 ANSWERS**

| | | | |
|---|---|---|---|
| 1 | many | 6 | much |
| 2 | much | 7 | much |
| 3 | many | 8 | many |
| 4 | much (money) | 9 | much |
| 5 | much | 10 | much |

NOTES:

1  Only three of these words are countable:

*times* = occasions
(as opposed to *time* = hours, days, months)

*staff* = people (plural although no 's')

programs: *software* (which is uncountable) is an adjective in this sentence

2  *much* by itself (4) = money

3  In 5 and 6 you have to search for the noun which much applies to — *equipment* and *work*.

**5** Monitor and correct as necessary. If students are weak on this, drill the words, e.g.,

*How many times?* — only a few
*How much time?* — only a little
*How many staff?* — only a few

## Speaking

Give students time to read the background information, then check with 'Many a Slip' (see page 28):

*You are consulting an American hard drink company. They are planning to introduce you to a physics teacher in your home. It is already successful in us where it is intended as a replacement for sports people. The company are dismissing you as consultants to help them position the product on the shelves. You have done some market research and now you are going.*

What does *break into* mean in the title? (*Get market share in a market which is new to you*)

**1** Give students time to study the charts. Check understanding if necessary. Elicit the most interesting findings for the purposes of this activity, e.g.,

*Most people buy sports drinks because they like the taste. Nearly three-quarters of all adults in the 14–17 age group buy sports drinks.*

**2** You could use the same examples and complete them with recommendations, e.g.,

*Most people buy sports drinks because they like the taste, so I suggest that you emphasize the fruity taste in your advertising.*

or:

*Nearly three-quarters of all adults in the 14–17 age group buy sports drinks so I recommend that you concentrate on the teenage market.*

**3 and 4**    See Student's Book. If appropriate give a new scenario for the listeners: you are bankers deciding which product to invest in. Decide which group gave the best presentation.

CLOSURE: Follow the procedure on page 11.